Champions of the Truth

Champions of
the Truth

Fundamentalism,
Modernism, and the
Maritime Baptists

G . A .   R A W L Y K

*The 1987–88 Winthrop Pickard
Bell Lectures in Maritime Studies*

Published for the
Centre for Canadian Studies
Mount Allison University
by
McGill-Queen's University Press
Montreal & Kingston • London • Buffalo

© Centre for Canadian Studies 1990
ISBN 0-7735-0760-4 (cloth)
ISBN 0-7735-0783-3 (paper)

Legal deposit second quarter 1990
Bibliothèque nationale du Québec

Printed in Canada on acid-free paper

This book has been published with the help of a
grant from the Winthrop Pickard Bell Maritime
Studies Fund.

Canadian Cataloguing in Publication Data

Rawlyk, George A., 1935–
  Champions of the truth
  "The 1987–1988 Winthrop Pickard Bell lectures in
  Maritime studies".
  Includes bibliographical references.
  ISBN 0-7735-0760-4 (bound) –
  ISBN 0-7735-0783-3 (pbk.)
  1. Baptists – Maritime Provinces – History. 2. Mod-
  ernist-fundamentalist controversy.   I. Mount Allison
  University. Centre for Canadian studies.   II. Title.
  BX6252.M37R39 1990   286'.715   C90-090003-2

Contents

Preface

In the fall of 1959, I began my university teaching career at Mount Allison University. During my two year sojourn in Sackville, I became more and more interested in the history of the Maritimes. This interest gradually evolved into a scholarly preoccupation with the New England-Nova Scotia-Acadia relationship in the seventeenth and eighteenth centuries. After 1985, however, my research interest shifted, this time to the religious history of the Maritimes in the 1920s and 1930s in general, and the Baptists in particular. I was significantly influenced by George Marsden's *Fundamentalism and American Culture: The Shaping of Twentieth-Century Evangelicalism 1870–1925*, first published in 1980, and I was determined to try to discover why, during the interwar years, the Maritime Baptist Convention, unlike its mainline Baptist counterparts in Central and Western Canada, did not experience a bitter and personal fundamentalist-modernist schism.

I hoped that my new research would throw some light on the essential contours of the Maritime Baptist experience in the 1920s and 1930s. But, of course, I did not want to look at the interwar years in splendid isolation. It was my aim to try to link the twentieth-century Maritime Baptist experience not only to its late eighteenth-century evangelical past but also to evolving events and personalities in the rest of Canada. Just when my research strategy was clicking into fragile place, late in 1986, I received an invitation from Mount Allison University to occupy the Winthrop Pickard Bell Chair in Maritime Studies for the 1987-88 academic year. Here was a marvellous opportunity, I thought, for me to begin serious work on my new research project and to try to find answers to a number of

questions that were beginning to perplex and intrigue me. For example, why did the Maritime Convention Baptists *not* have a serious
split in the 1920s and 1930s? Why was the convention so liberal and
accommodating to a variety of theologies during these years? Why
was Acadia University, the Baptist institution of higher learning,
more liberal than McMaster University, the Baptist institution whose
so-called modernist streak had precipitated a major schism in Baptist
ranks in Ontario and Quebec in the 1920s? Why was the Social
Gospel such a significant force in the Maritime Baptist Convention
throughout the 1920s and 1930s? How important was the evangelical–New Light tradition of the late eighteenth century and the nineteenth century in shaping the collective Maritime Baptist mind of
the interwar years and beyond?

My Bell lectures at Mount Allison University in late 1987 and early
1988 gave me the opportunity to address some of these questions.
And the response to these lectures, which I gave in modified form
in other parts of the Atlantic region, helped me to clarify my thinking
and strengthen my resolve to work in this area. In addition, I discovered that a number of people who heard my lectures or else
heard about them had in their possession extremely valuable primary sources about the twentieth-century Maritime Baptist experience. I was sent, for example, scores of letters and other documents
about the Reverend J.J. Sidey, a Maritime Baptist fundamentalist
leader I was very interested in, by his daughter who is now living
in Clementsport, Nova Scotia.

My Bell lectures, it is clear, are largely preliminary probes – what
some of my colleagues at Queen's University would call "think
pieces." It is my hope that eventually they will lead to a major study
dealing with the Baptist experience in the Maritimes in the first half
of the twentieth century.

While at Mount Allison University during the 1987-88 academic
year I benefited tremendously from the intellectual stimulation provided by Professor Larry McCann, the director of Canadian Studies.
Larry gave me support and encouragement when they were necessary; he also gave me friendship and wisdom. His wife Susan
showed me what warm hospitality really was. And for this I shall
always be grateful.

In addition, I benefited a great deal from my many contacts with
a first-rate scholar of eighteenth-century Nova Scotia and a good

friend, Dr Bill Godfrey, Dean of Arts at Mount Allison, who welcomed me to his fourth-year honours seminar on Atlantic Canada. Professor Marty Davis, of the Department of History, kindly invited me to participate in his seminar dealing with religion and Canada. I probably learned more than he realized from this class.

My return to Mount Allison, in the autumn of 1987, closed an academic circle which had begun there in 1959. I owe more than most people realize to Mount Allison University and remain very proud of my association with "Mt A."

Foreword

Champions of the Truth: Fundamentalism, Modernism, and the Maritime Baptists is a remarkable volume. It is by no means a comprehensive statement of the subject (and Professor Rawlyk would be the first to admit to its incompleteness). There are a number of pithy, challenging, but unsubstantiated claims that consequently infuriate (but which are nonetheless probably quite accurate). One might also wish to know more about the experience of other religious groups as they came to grips with the modernists and their theology. These minor annoyances aside, the essays are remarkable because they draw our attention to a neglected area of the Maritime past in a manner that forces us to reconsider our approach and attitudes to understanding that past. There is a clarion call to arms; a plea to stop ignoring the religious dimension of the region's history. Not unexpectedly, the plea is backed up by essays that are persuasive to the cause. After reading these essays, it seems clear that any future interpretation of Maritime history would be incomplete without a full discussion of non-secular forces. Although a "Whig bias" has diverted our attention, the religious factor – as in Puritan New England, Catholic New France, or the Pentecostal "New" South – is far too important to neglect. Since the renaissance of Maritime history began officially with the publication of *Acadiensis* in 1972, the largest corpus of research has focused on economic, political, and (to a lesser degree) social matters. The cultural factor has been, for the most part, either downplayed or ignored. But this can no longer occur, and we should be in Professor Rawlyk's debt for chiding our neglect.

The essays are also remarkable because they constantly provoke. To me, the underlying structure of Professor Rawlyk's writing centres on dialectical analysis. There is little middle ground in the presentation of an argument, which typically focuses on personalities, forces; or causes that stand in opposition to one another. Particular themes are therefore played out in expositions of opposition: individualism vs community; insider vs outsider; revivalists vs the status quo; the Maritime periphery vs the Ontario centre; and, of course, endorsing the book's title, fundamentalism vs modernism. Central to Professor Rawlyk's dialectical approach are the actions of individuals, which breathe life's tensions into the web of the religious and historical experience. There is the bifurcated personality of the fundamentalist T. T. Shield ("angelic look"/"traces of the demonic"); the pairing of J. J. Sidey and J. B. Daggett ("their respective strengths complemented one another"); and the competitive evangelical zeal of the "New Light" Henry Alline and the Methodist itinerant Freeborn Garrettson. The presentation of opposites provokes, forcing us to consider first one side and then the other, but our conclusions and those of Professor Rawlyk are never simplistic statements cast solely in black or in white.

Firmly rooted in a theoretical base, the explanations that flow from the dialectical approach owe much to Anthony Wallace's "revitalization" process of the religious experience; to Victor Turner's "world of self-discovery and inner freedom"; and to George Marsden's emphasis on self-exposition in historical writing. Concepts and events are therefore placed solidly in context. Well-illustrating Professor Rawlyk's analytical skills are the theoretical reasoning and empirical research that lie behind the story of the conflict between fundamentalists and modernists in the Maritime Baptist Church in the 1920s and 1930s. This account demonstrates clearly that religious history need not be dogmatic, institutionally bound, or of little consequence to our understanding of regional cultures or their social structures. Quite the contrary, we are presented with meaningful explanations that reveal much that is essential to our search for the Maritime identity. We learn, in provocative fashion, that religious traditions and disputes define a unique Maritime religious culture. In the case of the Maritime Baptists in the 1920s and 1930s, for example, their view of religious matters remained much more tolerant of liberal (modernist) doctrine than that of the Baptists of Ontario, Quebec, or Western Canada. The fact that the powerful T. T. Shields could do little to influence this liberal stance is itself an interesting revelation. Economic forces might place the region in servitude, but religious values (witness also the enduring strength of Presbyterianism in the region) were harder to centralize.

Finally, the essays are remarkable because they reveal first hand the developing thoughts and on-going reflections of a mature historian. We are treated to the all-too-rare occurrence of a scholar admitting that some of his arguments have fallen short of the mark and need to be challenged and revised. But by whom? By the original proponent, of course. Thus within the three essays we are provoked by plausible arguments, then provoked again by the author's own revisions. We finish our reading of these essays not only better informed about the religious dimension of the Maritimes' history but interested in taking up the challenge of adding to that understanding.

George Rawlyk is a gifted historian, and his contributions over the past three decades to our understanding of the Maritime past and present have been outstanding. For these and other reasons of scholarly excellence, Professor Rawlyk was invited to hold the Winthrop Pickard Bell Chair in Maritime Studies at Mount Allison University in 1987–88. For those of us who spent time with George during his visit, it was a memorable year; George gave unstintingly of his time and energy to visit classes, to advise students and staff, and to lecture widely throughout the region. But it was also clear that the Chair offered George an opportunity to engage in research, to reflect, and to write at a pace that would lead to a truly remarkable output of new and original interpretations of the Maritime past. At the heart of this writing experience was a renewed interest and focus on the religious history of the Maritimes, in particular on the place of the Baptists in the social and cultural heritage of the region. The immediate expression of this research, reflection, and writing are the Bell Lectures published here, delivered on three occasions during the 1987–88 academic year.

Mount Allison and the wider academic community have been well served by George Rawlyk's tenure as Winthrop Pickard Bell Professor of Maritime Studies.

Larry McCann
Davidson Professor
of Canadian Studies

Champions of the Truth

1 Revivalism and the Maritime Religious Experience

Religious conversions have, in the past, actually occurred; peoples' lives have been profoundly and permanently changed – sometimes gradually and sometimes suddenly and traumatically. Conversions still take place, as do religious revivals – spiritual awakenings involving often large numbers of men, women, and children. In fact, since the 1770s, tens of thousands of Maritimers have been deeply affected by the religious revivals which, like epidemics, have swept through entire communities, sometimes entire regions, and once or twice entire provinces. Yet, despite the frequency and intensity of some of the revivals that have occurred over a two hundred year period, and despite the remarkable number of people touched directly or indirectly by them, surprisingly little has been written about the revivals by Canadian religious scholars. It is as though the revivals and the revivalists who have helped coax these often large-scale social movements into existence have been relegated to some dark and distant corner of historical oblivion by the shapers of the Canadian historical tradition. It is understandable, perhaps, why so many secular historians have been, and remain, either indifferent or hostile to the Protestant revivalist tradition and all that it represents. They look at the Canadian past in general, and the Maritime past in particular, largely through a secular lens carefully ground both by a suspicion and opposition to most things religious, with the result that they see what they want to see – especially what seems relevant to them today. A significant presentist bias, it may be argued, shapes their research methodology and their results. Working-class scholars and feminists, for example, as well as the more traditional scholars, drill into the past in order to try to explain some contemporary concern. They are, furthermore, encouraged to do so by funding agencies preoccupied with what the Canada Council and the sshrcc proudly refer to as "the social relevance" of financially supportable research.[1]

The secular and presentist bias of so much recent Canadian historical research and writing, as well as that of the major funding agencies, has, without question, deflected serious scholarly interest and concern away from Canadian religious history in general and what may be called the evangelical tradition in particular. The North American evangelical tradition since the eighteenth century, according to Professor Stephen Marini, is distinctive for its heavy emphasis on the "intense conversion experience, fervid piety, ecstatic worship forms, Biblical literalism, the pure church ideal, and charismatic leadership."[2] Each of these characteristics, it may be argued, is seen by the new secular priests as an embarrassing relic of the pre-modern age. The evangelical tradition, moreover, seems to have far too much in common with contemporary fundamentalism, especially its peculiar American TV variant, and few Canadian scholars want to be found guilty by any association with such a movement – with good reason. To study the evangelical tradition seriously, objectively, and with empathy is often viewed as a closed-minded acceptance of the fundamentalist position and an irrational betrayal of all that is good, progressive, and open-minded – in other words, a betrayal of all that is perceived to be scholarly.

One can understand but not necessarily condone the secular bias of so much recent Canadian historical writing. Yet, one wonders why those few scholars who regard themselves as evangelicals, or at least as sympathetic to the evangelical position, are apparently so indifferent to the evangelical historical tradition. Perhaps they are indifferent to the past because they feel intuitively that it has nothing of value to contribute to the present. Perhaps they are suspicious of the past because they fear that it might, in fact, embarrass them. Perhaps some lack the necessary scholarly skills to scrape into the deep recesses of past events and personalities. Or maybe their simple, providential approach to history – what some critics have called the "shower-of-blessings approach" – makes serious historical writing basically redundant. There may be other reasons as well, such as a conviction that so-called conservative biblical scholarship is far more important in protecting the pristine evangelical faith than is historical writing about what, to many, is an irrelevant evangelical historical tradition. According to at least one influential Canadian evangelical, H.H. Budd, the president of Briercrest Bible College in Saskatchewan, true evangelicals in Canada are – as he once cogently put it – "much busier in making history than in writing it."[3] In other words, many evangelical scholars want to devote their time and energy to bringing about conversions rather than to researching what is, to them, some obscure revival or revivalist of the distant past.

Obviously, there are many good reasons why there has been so little serious historical research done about the evangelical tradition in Canada, and why so much – so very much – still needs to be done. An important part of the evangelical tradition, and one that has in recent years particularly interested me, has been revivalism. In my writing about Canadian religious revivals and revivalists, as any careful analysis of my recent work will clearly show, I have been significantly influenced by three American scholars – Anthony Wallace and his revitalization thesis, Victor Turner and his *Ritual Process*, and George Marsden, through his work on American evangelicals and fundamentalism. Wallace and Turner are influential social anthropologists and Marsden is, without question, one of the leading American religious historians.

During the last quarter of the eighteenth century two remarkably gifted charismatic preachers crisscrossed the Maritimes preaching their own particular versions of the radical evangelical message. Both were American-born; both were converted at approximately the same time; both, though not Baptists, had a profound impact on the Baptist denomination in the Maritimes; both were ardent advocates of Free Will as opposed to Calvinism; and both believed enthusiastically in a religion of the heart *and* the head. Moreover, both evangelists also encouraged the growth of Methodism in the Maritimes and both eventually died in the United States. They both believed in the efficacy of religious revivals and the central importance of the New Birth. They both encouraged their thousands of listeners to follow them – to the peak of religious ecstasy – so that they too could become part of Christ's spirituality and perfectability. Both men – Henry Alline and Freeborn Garrettson – established a revivalistic paradigm which would become the evangelical norm in the Maritimes for Baptists, Methodists, and Congregationalists alike, well into the twentieth century. And their revivalistic legacy is still found in the more isolated areas of the region, even today. It should be no surprise, therefore, that Reginald Bibby, in his recently published *Fragmented Gods: The Poverty and Potential of Religion in Canada*, has argued that in the 1980s the Atlantic region is "the nation's true Bible Belt."[4]

In recent years Henry Alline has, according to at least one scholar, become a "Canadian religious Paul Bunyan."[5] He is now widely regarded as a spiritual giant of a man, who singlehandedly breathed a colony-wide revival into existence and then permanently shaped the religious contours of the Maritime region. Most of Alline's contemporaries saw him as Nova Scotia's George Whitefield – as a powerful instrument of the Almighty, a truly charismatic and uniquely spiritual man, and the person responsible for the series of religious revivals that swept the colony during the American Revolution. Historians and other scholars in the nineteenth and twentieth centuries have been, almost to a person, impressed by Alline's mystical theology, his creative powers, and his unusual ability to communicate to others his profound sense of Christian ecstasy.[6] Some scholars have regarded him as the "prophet" of Nova Scotia's so-called First Great Awakening and as a "flaming evangelist" who channelled the religious enthusiasm he had helped to create in Nova Scotia during the American Revolution into "neutrality."[7] Others have seen him either as an "intellectual and literary giant"[8] who significantly marked the Canadian pietistic tradition or as a charismatic preacher who provided confused, disoriented Nova Scotians with a special sense of collective identity and a powerful "sense of mission" at a critical moment in their historical development.[9] And, according to Professor David Bell of the University of New Brunswick, Alline – taking into account both his immediate and long-term impact on the Maritimes – "stands unrivalled as the greatest Canadian of the eighteenth Century, the greatest Maritimer of any age and the most significant religious figure this country has yet produced."[10]

Henry Alline was born in Newport, Rhode Island, in 1748 and moved with his parents to Falmouth, in the Minas Basin region of Nova Scotia, in 1760. Like most young people in the settlement, he was brought up in a pious and Calvinist atmosphere. There was little in his rural upbringing in Nova Scotia to suggest that Alline would develop into the province's most gifted preacher and most prolific hymn-writer. He was known in his community – at least until his conversion – only for his outgoing personality and his skill in "the art of tanning and currying."[11]

In the early months of 1775, the then twenty-seven-year-old Alline experienced a profound spiritual and psychological crisis, the resolution of which provided the key turning-point in his life. Alline's conversion – his traumatic New Birth – was significantly shaped by a finely developed morbid introspection, a fear of imminent death, and by the considerable pressure he felt during the early months of the American revolutionary struggle to commit himself one way or another.

The sudden, transforming power of spiritual regeneration – the New Light New Birth – compelled Alline to declare these emotionally charged words, which would remain the cutting-edge of his Christian message until his death in 1784: "O the infinite condescension of God to a worm of the dust! For though my whole soul was filled with love, and ravished with a divine ecstasy beyond any doubts or fears, or thoughts of being then deceived, for I enjoyed a heaven on earth, and it seemed as if I were wrapped up in God."[12]

Over and over again in his *Journal*, as well as in his published sermons and pamphlets and his hymns and spiritual songs, Alline referred to his having been "ravished" by the "divine ecstasy" and "married" to his Saviour by the redeeming power of the Holy Spirit. Divine love had overwhelmed him to such an extent in 1775 that he began to view his own experience as the pattern for all other regeneration experiences. It is not surprising, therefore, that Alline expected his followers to share the intense ecstasy of spiritual rapture – the central New Light experience – which he had experienced and which he regarded as being the only satisfactory means of true regeneration.[13]

Not only was Alline a remarkably charismatic preacher and a controversial essayist, he was also an unusually gifted hymn writer. He composed over five hundred hymns and spiritual songs containing the simplified essence of his evangelistic message. Alline used "sensuous imagery, subjectivism, and Biblical paraphrase"[14] in his hymns to communicate deep religious truths to those who sang and listened to them. Alline's hymns and spiritual songs articulated religious language ordinary folk could understand and resonate with, for they "represented the common denominator of plain-folk religious belief"[15] and they captured superbly the simple essence of the Christian message. Repetition, the use of striking phrases, the creative linking of lyrics to popular folk-tunes – these elements helped drill the fundamental Christian beliefs into the inner consciousness of those who sang or listened to Alline's hymns and spiritual songs and made the experience unforgettable.

The core of Alline's New Light–evangelical theology, it should be stressed, is to be found in his more than five hundred hymns, which he wrote during the latter part of his life. On the whole, these are powerful and evocative hymns, and for many of the inhabitants of Nova Scotia and New England during and after the revolutionary war, they contained the essential truths of the Christian gospel. Alline himself acknowledged that his use of graphic language "alarmed" the heart and "stirred" it "up to action, by local objects or vocal sounds."[16] The flavour of Alline's hymns and spiritual songs is captured in the following hymns, which were especially loved by his followers:

Dark and distressing was the day,
When o'er the dismal gulf I lay,
With trembling knees and stutt'ring breath
I shudder'd on the brink of death.

Destruction yawn'd on ev'ry side,
I saw no refuge where to hide,
Ten thousand foes beset me round,
No friend nor comforter I found.

I groan'd and cry'd, while torn with grief,
But none appear'd for my relief,
'Till Christ the Saviour passing by,
Look'd on me with a pitying eye.

He brought me from the gates of hell,
The wonders of his grace to tell
O may he now inspire my tongue
To make his lovely name my song.[17]

And, in a hymn entitled "A Miracle of Grace," Alline portrayed his own conversion experience in an attempt to appeal to others:

No mortal tongue can ever tell,
The horrors of that gloomy night,
When I hung o'er that brink of hell,
Expecting soon my wretched flight!

I felt my burden waste my life,
While guilt did ev'ry hope devour,
Trembling I stretch'd with groans and strife
For to escape the dreadful hour.

But in the midst of all my grief,
The great Messiah spoke in love;
His arm appeared for my relief,
And bid my guilt and sorrow move.

He pluck'd me from the jaws of hell,
With his almighty arm of pow'r;
And O! no mortal tongue can tell,
The change of that immortal hour!

Then I enjoy'd a sweet release,
From chains of sin and pow'rs of death,
My soul was fill'd with heav'nly peace,
My groans were turn'd to praising breath.[18]

For Alline, regeneration made – as he once put it – "Heaven on earth" not only a possibility for the believer but a reality:

Some happy days I find below
When Jesus is with me;
Nor would I any pleasure know
O Jesus but in thee.

When I can taste immortal love,
And find my Jesus near,
My soul is blest where e'er I rove,
I neither mourn nor fear.

Let angels boast their joys above,
I taste the same below,

They drink of the Redeemer's love,
And I have Jesus too. [19]

In an especially memorable hymn entitled "The great love of Christ display'd in his death," Alline captured what he considered to be the core of his mystical, conversion experience. Many of his followers must have found in Alline's vivid description the emotional power of their own unique experiences and often used his language to describe their personal New Birth.

As near to Calvary I pass
Me thinks I see a bloody cross.
Where a poor victim hangs;
His flesh with ragged irons tore,
His limbs all dress'd with purple gore,
Gasping in dying pangs.

Surpriz'd the spectacle to see,
I ask'd who can this victim be,
In such exquisite pain?
Why thus consign'd to woes I cry'd?
"*Tis I*, the bleeding God reply'd,
To save a world from sin."

A god for rebel mortals dies!
How can it be, my soul replies!
What! Jesus die for me!
"*Yes, saith the suff'ring Son of God,
I give my life, I spill my blood.
For thee, poor soul, for thee.*"

Lord since thy life thou'st freely giv'n,
To bring my wretched soul to heav'n.
And bless me with thy love;
Then to thy feet, O God, I'll fall,
Give thee my life, my soul, my all,
To reign with thee above.

All other lovers I'll adieu,
My dying lover I'll pursue,

And bless the slaughter'd Lamb;
My life, my strength, my voice and days,
I will devote to wisdom's ways,
And sound his bleeding fame.

And when this tott'ring life shall cease,
I'll leave these mortal climes in peace,
And soar to realms of light;
There where my heav'nly lover reigns,
I'll join to raise immortal strains,
All ravish'd with delight.[20]

Alline's hymns are still sung in a few Baptist churches in New Brunswick and Nova Scotia. They are not found in hymn-books but in the amazing memories of scores of worshippers who, even today, regard themselves as disciples of Henry Alline. Alline's hymns are an integral part of an oral culture that still exists in the upper reaches of the Saint John River Valley of New Brunswick and in the Yarmouth region of Nova Scotia. Few may now have any knowledge of his printed sermons or treatises or have seen his *Journal*, but they do remember something from Alline's *Hymns and Spiritual Songs*, perhaps the most lasting legacy of his all too brief sojourn in what his followers frequently referred to as "this vale of tears."[21]

Even though Alline's *Hymns and Spiritual Songs* is extremely significant in terms of the Falmouth evangelist's legacy not only to Maritime religious culture but also to North American religious life, it was his remarkable charismatic preaching which gave shape and substance to Nova Scotia's First Great Awakening. His two published theological books obviously did not. The *Two Mites on Some of the Most Important and much disputed Points of Divinity* (Halifax, 1781) and *The Anti-Traditionalist* (Halifax, 1783) were not widely read in the colony. If anything, his *Two Mites* – a convoluted anti-Calvinist work permeated by what Maurice Armstrong once referred to as "Alline's peculiar doctrines"[22] – probably helped to dampen the revival fire. Nevertheless these two books tell us a great deal about Alline's theology which, according to one contemporary, was a peculiar mixture of "Calvinism, Antinomianism and Enthusiasm."[23] But the *Two Mites* and *The Anti-Traditionalist*, both of which are full of "rhetorical and extravagant"[24] views, shed little real light on the awakening, and on Alline's charismatic powers. Alline's *Journal*, however, does. (The *Journal* was not published until 1806 even though a manuscript version of the document was in circulation among Alline's followers soon after his death in February 1784.) The *Journal* provides a superb introspective and illuminating account of the spiritual travails of this unusually gifted eighteenth-century North-American mystic and preacher.[25] There is in the *Journal* a remarkable and almost exaggerated tension between the mystical, pietistic, and inward looking Alline and the charismatic evangelist determined to preach the gospel in every corner of Nova Scotia and New England.

Alline's *Journal* contains a number of evocative descriptions of Nova Scotia's First Great Awakening. Alline describes, for example, his visit to Liverpool in November 1782:

Almost all the town assembled together, and some that were lively christians prayed and exhorted, and God was there with a truth. I preached every day, and sometimes twice a day; and the houses where I went were crowded almost all the time. Many were brought out of darkness and rejoiced, and exhorted in public. And O how affecting it was to see some young people not only exhort their companions, but also take their parents by the hand, and entreat them for their soul's sake to rest no longer in their sins, but fly to Jesus Christ while there was hope. One young lad (who turned out to be a very bright christian) I saw, after sermon, take his father by the hand, and cry out, "O father, you have been a great sinner, and now are an old man: an old sinner, with grey hairs upon your head, going right down to destruction. O turn, turn, dear father, return and fly to Jesus Christ": with many other such like expressions and entreaties, enough to melt a stony heart. The work of God continued with uncommon power through almost all the place. But the small number that did not fall in with the work were raging and scoffing, and some blaspheming.[26]

During late December 1782 and much of January and early February 1783, Alline continued to pour oil on the revival fires in the Liverpool region. In early January he sailed to Halifax, with two of his Liverpool sermons in his pocket, to make arrangements with the printer, Anthony Henry, to have them published. Alline detested Halifax, regarding Haligonians "in general ... almost as dark and as vile as in Sodom."[27] After spending ten days in the Nova Scotia capital, Alline was delighted to return to Liverpool, where he found

– as he so characteristically expressed it – "the waters troubled, and souls stepping in." He felt inspired to declare:

O the happy days which I there enjoyed, not only in my own soul, but to see the kingdom of God *flourishing*. When I went to preach at the meeting house, at the hour appointed, the people were crowding to hear; and when the sermon was over, I was obliged to stop many hours in the broad-alley, to discourse with the people; for it seemed as if they could not go away. While I was there this last time, the christians gathered together in fellowship by telling their experiences and getting fellowship one for another; and so joined in a body, separating themselves from the world.[28]

On Sunday, 16 February 1783, Alline preached his last sermon in Liverpool. Simon Perkins, a member of the congregation, recorded in his diary this sensitive description of the community's reaction. "Mr. Alline Preached both parts of the day & Evening. A Number of People made a Relation of their Experiences after the Meeting was concluded & Expressed Great Joy & Comfort in what god had done for them."[29] For Perkins, Alline's revival had the same "appearance" as New England's First Great Awakening. Perkins, like most of his Nova Scotia Yankee contemporaries, saw Alline as part of the New Light–evangelical movement. Perkins never mentioned Alline's so-called heterodox views but praised instead the "wonderful ... Spirit of God moving upon the people."[30] Other Nova Scotia Yankees made precisely the same point. When confronted by the anti-Alline minister, the Reverend Jonathan Scott, Amos Hilton, a leading member of the Congregation Church in Yarmouth, declared that a preacher's theology was really of secondary importance. Hilton replied to Scott's vicious critique of Alline's perceived heretical views that it was "no Matter of any great Consequence to him what a Man's Principles were, if he was but earnest in promoting a good Work."[31] As had been the case in New England's First Great Awakening "the manner in which a preacher delivered his message was often more revealing of his persuasion that the particular doctrines he happened to espouse."[32] Preachers were viewed as being special instruments of the Almighty not because of the defensive religious orthodoxy they articulated but because they could trigger religious revivals into existence. The words they uttered were not nearly as important as the New Birth produced. Moreover, as the noted French author La Rochefoucauld once perceptively observed: "Enthusiasm is the most convincing orator: it is like the functioning of an infallible law of nature. The simplest man, fired with enthusiasm, is more persuasive than the most eloquent without it."[33]

Alline's sermons, of course, must be viewed in the context of his times, his theology, and his own personality. He probably preached more than fifteen hundred extemporaneous sermons as he criss-crossed Nova Scotia between 1777 and 1783. Alline did not have the time to prepare sermons; he preached as the Spirit moved him. He had learned quickly how to move his listeners by using language they could understand – earthy, sexual, simple, evocative, and often powerful language. He knew instinctively how to link words to create literary images that drilled into the human mind, by first transforming doubt into agony and then transforming agony into intense spiritual relief. For Alline, as had been the case for Augustine centuries earlier, effective preaching was the "ministry of the tongue," whereby the preacher "succeeded in putting Christ in the worshipper's ears." Sometimes his preaching, "charged with emotionalism" as it was and delivered in a "fervent and eloquent manner" in a resonating tenor voice, became superb poetry. Sometimes, the poetry was sung as a spiritual song and followed immediately by an almost frenzied outburst of words directed at specific people in his audience. This too was an important characteristic of Alline's preaching. He loved to direct certain themes in his sermons at certain people – at the young and the old, at fishermen, community leaders and soldiers. People who heard Alline must have felt that he was preaching especially *to* them and *at* them, and hundreds responded positively to this form of directed intimacy.[34]

Alline's preaching, the evidence suggests, was permeated by a preoccupation with disintegrating, disintegrated, and renewed relationships. Generalizing from his own conversion, Alline emphasized that every Nova Scotian could emulate him if only they reached out, in faith, to Christ. In a world where traditional relationships were falling apart, a personal "interest in Christ" created by the New Birth, as Alline put it, was the means whereby threatened relationships would be strengthened. Conversion was perceived by Alline and his followers as the short-circuiting of a complex process – a short-circuiting which produced instant satisfaction, solace, and intense relief. The Awakening was, in one sense, a collection of these positive individual experiences; it helped give shape and substance to a new and distinct Nova Scotia sense of identity. And it was Alline's powerfully charismatic and evangelical preaching, and not his published work, that would shape the contours of the First Great Awakening.

There is a simple gravestone on Alline's grave in the cemetery near the Congregational Church in North Hampton, New Hampshire. It is difficult to read the inscription and few people now try to do so. The original inscription reads:

> The Reverend Henry Alline
> of Falmouth, Nova Scotia,
> in the midst of his zealous
> travels in the cause of Christ,
> languished on the way, and
> cheerfully resigned his life
> at North Hampton, 2 Feb. 1784,
> in the 35 year of his age,
> whose remains are here interred.

Sometime after 1784 one of Alline's relatives added the following sentence to the gravestone:

> He was burning and a shining light
> and justly esteemed the Apostle
> of Nova Scotia.[35]

A little more than a year after Henry Alline's death in New Hampshire on 2 February 1784, an intense religious revival swept through many of the Yankee settlements of Nova Scotia. It was a revival which owed a great deal to an extraordinarily able Methodist preacher from Maryland, Freeborn Garrettson. And it was a revival, moreover, which energized a weakened New Light–evangelical movement by, among other things, providing it with a coterie of new, young, energetic, and remarkably gifted leaders, the most outstanding of whom were Edward Manning, Joseph Dimock, Harris Harding, and Theodore Seth Harding.[36] These men would become the "patriarchs" of the Maritime Baptist Church.

Freeborn Garrettson, who would trigger the first post-Alline revival, and his American Methodist associate, the frail James Oliver Cromwell, sailed from New York for Nova Scotia in the middle of

February 1785. After a particularly stormy passage, they arrived in Halifax. The two young American Methodist itinerants had been "set apart for Nova Scotia" by the leaders of the American Methodist Episcopal Church who had been under considerable pressure from John Wesley and also from William Black, the Nova Scotia Methodist leader, to provide missionary assistance at a critical time in the colony's history.[37] The death of Alline had created a religious vacuum in what is now Nova Scotia. And the sudden arrival in the late 1770s and early 1780s of approximately twenty thousand Loyalists,[38] some of whom were Methodists, provided both a new mission field and also the means whereby Black, in particular, hoped the Yankee, New Light hegemony over much of the colony could finally be broken. What Black had failed to accomplish in his face-to-face confrontations with Alline during the late 1770s and early 1780s, he hoped visiting American itinerants might accomplish in his beloved Nova Scotia.

It should be kept in mind that during the years immediately following the end of the American War of Independence, many in Nova Scotia experienced a disconcerting collective sense of acute disorientation and confusion. As was the case in neighbouring northern New England, hundreds of "common people were cut loose from all sorts of traditional bonds and found themselves freer, more independent, more unconstrained than ever before in their history."[39] The arrival of the Loyalists to peninsular Nova Scotia at the end of the Revolution seemed to accelerate a process of social disintegration already underway in some regions of the colony. The Loyalists, according to Edward Manning, the influential Baptist patriarch, had a "bad and ... dreadful" effect on the colony since they "corrupted" societal values and made many Nova Scotians "adepts in wickedness."[40] Thus, as Professor Gordon Wood has argued, "traditional structures of authority crumbled under the momentum of the Revolution, and common people increasingly discovered that they no longer had to accept the old distinctions" that had driven them into a widely perceived subservient and vulnerable status.[41] And, as might have been expected, "bizarre but emotionally satisfying ways of relating to God and others" became increasingly widespread as many Nova Scotians sought a renewed sense of "community-belonging" in order to neutralize the powerful forces of alienation then sweeping the colony. It was a period when, it has been perceptively observed, "everything was believable" and almost "everything could be doubted."[42] "Radical enthusiasts and visionaries," regarding themselves as the disciples of Henry Alline and as propagators of his tradition, became the "advanced guard" of the renewed "popular evangelical movement with which they shared a common hostility to orthodox authority."[43] By 1790 these radical New Lights, as they were spitefully referred to by their enemies, were a people in a delicate state of spiritual tension, "poised like a steel spring by the contradicting forces pulling within it." There was a mystical quality permeating their belief system and also a secular one; there was a democratic bias and also an authoritarian one; there was an individualism, as well as a tendency towards a sense of community. For some, the seemingly contradictory forces within the New-Light mind would soon neutralize one another, producing apathy, indifference, and disenchantment. A significant number of others expected the dynamic tension to result in a renewed pietism and to become a crucial link in the chain connecting Henry Alline's First Great Awakening with Nova Scotia's Second Awakening, in which New Lights and Methodists were particularly active. And an influential minority, known as the "new dispensationalists" by friends and enemies alike, found that the state of spiritual tension brought about by the arrival of the Loyalists, the Garrettsonian revival, the continuing influence of Alline's legacy, and the growing American sectarian influences provided a heaven-sent opportunity to stretch Alline's gospel beyond the boundaries of evangelical orthodoxy – especially in the early 1790s.[44]

Soon after landing in Halifax, Garrettson had elbowed William Black aside and become the most influential Methodist leader in Nova Scotia. Garrettson was regarded, with some justification, as a "man of varied resources, a powerful preacher and capable organizer, of genuine piety and holiness of life, who left an abiding impression on the whole life of the province."[45] "It may be fairly questioned" claimed his biographer Nathan Bangs, "whether any one minister in the Methodist Episcopal Church, or indeed in any other Church, has been instrumental in the awakening and conversion of more sinners than Garrettson."[46] Garrettson was, without question, an unusually gifted minister; he was a powerful, some would say charismatic, preacher; he was, moreover, an indefatigable itinerant and a man almost obsessed with – as he once cogently expressed it in Wesleyan language – "rising higher and higher in the divine image."[47] Though he spent only twenty-six months in Nova Scotia, Garrettson "left an abiding impression on the whole life of the province."[48] Next to Henry Alline, the evidence suggests, the Maryland Methodist was probably the most able and influential Protestant preacher in eighteenth-century or nineteenth-century Nova Scotia.

Garrettson was born on 15 August 1752 in Harford County, Maryland, near the mouth of the Susquehanna River.[49] His father, an active Anglican, was a wealthy slaveholder who was also opposed to Methodism, considering it a pernicious manifestation of sectarian enthusiasm. Though eager to please his father, soon after his twentieth birthday Garrettson fell under the influence of various itinerant Methodist preachers. And, in 1775, at approximately the same time that Alline was being converted in Nova Scotia, Garrettson experienced his own traumatic New Birth. After listening to a Methodist itinerant, and being under intense conviction, Garrettson, who was in the prime of life, became, as he expressed it, "for the first time, reconciled to the justice of God." According to the young Marylander: "The enmity of my heart was slain, and the plan of salvation was open to me. I saw a beauty in the perfections of the Deity, and felt that power of faith and love that I had been a stranger to. My soul was exceeding happy that I seemed as if I wanted to take wings and fly to heaven."[50] Garrettson became a Methodist circuit preacher in 1776, and only his death on 26 July 1827 brought about an end to what has been called the glorious "story of his long, heroic, and successful services in the itinerant ranks."[51]

It is noteworthy that, soon after his conversion, Garrettson felt compelled to free his slaves since he then regarded the institution of slavery as being the antithesis to his brand of evangelical Christianity. He began his Methodist ministerial work in 1776 as a preacher-on-trial and he itinerated widely for the next few years in Maryland and neighbouring states. A pacifist like Henry Alline, Garrettson wanted to have nothing to do with the American Revolution; he declared that "it was contrary to my mind, and grievous to my conscience, to have any hand in shedding human blood."[52] Consequently he pursued a policy of explicit neutrality, despite much persecution from the patriots. Garrettson was formally ordained a Methodist minister at the Baltimore Conference of December 1784, the conference at which the Methodist Episcopal Church of the United States formally came into being. Also during this conference, Garrettson was instructed to make his way to Nova Scotia – the British colony that had remained steadfastly loyal to the

British cause during the American Revolution. He was to live and work in Nova Scotia for only twenty-six months, but he had a tremendous impact there.

Garrettson was a man of amazing energy; this, together with his remarkable missionary zeal, helps to explain his results. For more than fifty years he preached his evangelical Methodist gospel from North Carolina to Nova Scotia, a period during which he was responsible for thousands of conversions – over twenty thousand some have claimed. Garrettson once described to Bishop Francis Asbury, his American superior, a "typical" week in Halifax: "Sunday eight o'clock preach in our little chapel, which will hold about four hundred persons; ten o'clock preach in the poor house, where there are about a hundred people; ... at twelve o'clock in the preaching house; four o'clock in a private house by the dockyard; and by candlelight in the chapel. I preach every night in the week. Friday visit the prisoners."[53] Garrettson did not mention his frequent house visits; the time spent in keeping up his correspondence with fellow Methodists in Nova Scotia, New Brunswick, Great Britain, and the United States; his "diligence and zeal" in studying the scriptures; and his exemplary "prayerfulness and watchfulness." He was, according to his biographer, the antithesis of "the slothful servant."[54]

During his brief stay in Nova Scotia, Garrettson visited virtually every settlement, apart from Pictou. A year before his death, Garrettson described his Nova Scotia experience:

I began to visit the towns, and to traverse the mountains and valleys, frequently on foot, with my knapsack at my back, up and down the Indian paths in the wilderness, when it was not expedient to take a horse; and I had often to wade through the mud and water of morasses, and frequently to satisfy my hunger from my knapsack, to quench my thirst from a brook, and rest my weary limbs on the leaves of trees. This was indeed going forth weeping; but thanks be to God, he compensated me for all my toil, for many precious souls were awakened and converted.[55]

Garrettson took full advantage of the earlier assiduous missionary labour of William Black, as well as that of Henry Alline and his itinerating disciples, men like John Payzant, Joseph Bailey, Thomas Handley Chipman, and Ebeneezer Hobbs (a teenage New Light exhorter). Not only did he cultivate the Yankee, New-Light heartland that stretched from Falmouth down the Annapolis Valley to

Granville, and from Yarmouth up the southern shore to Argyle, Liverpool, and Chester, he also broke important new missionary ground in the Loyalist centre of Shelburne.

Garrettson, like Alline, had a powerful voice but his was "harsh and high-pitched,"[56] a fact which did not impede its projection over a distance of "a quarter of a mile."[57] His preaching "focused on Christ, Heaven and Hell"[58] but always from a Methodist perspective which stressed the importance of human initiative in the conversion process. And, because of his genteel background, Garrettson was remarkedly successful in aiming his message not only at the so-called middling and lower sorts but also at society's leaders. However, it should not be assumed that Garrettson's background meant that he was suspicious of all forms of emotionalism. Nothing could have been further from the truth. Generalizing from his own very emotional conversion experience Garrettson once declared: "to suppose a work of grace without the excitement of human passions, is as great an absurdity as it would be to expect a man to breathe without any movements of the lungs."[59]

It is not surprising, therefore, that Garrettson touched such a responsive chord in those New-Light areas of Nova Scotia where Alline had experienced his most noteworthy successes – despite the opposition of some of the more extreme Allinites whom Garrettson called "as deluded a people as I ever saw."[60] These "Allinites" were Alline's disciples who were pushing his gospel towards Antinomianism – a belief that true Christians were not subject to any moral law. The Methodist preacher attracted large, attentive audiences in Nova Scotia in the spring of 1785. At Horton, on Sunday 22 May, over one hundred people turned out to hear him: "the General Cry was after preaching – if this is Methodist Doctrine, it is agreeable to truth."[61] Later that same day, in the New-Light centre of Cornwallis, there was, according to Garrettson, "a Considerable moving on ye hearts of ye people." And on the following day, after a particularly emotional meeting, there was a universal "cry ... if this is Methodist doctrine, I will be a Methodist." Scores of Yankees, some of whom had first been awakened by Whitefield and others by Alline, "after meeting ... continued some time hanging around each other, inquiring what they should do to be saved." Garrettson hoped that the revival would give the radical Allinites a fatal blow – what the Methodist preacher termed a "wonderful Stab."[62]

Preaching at a minimum three sermons each Sunday, either in barns, private homes, or Baptist and Presbyterian churches, and once each day of the week, Garrettson continued to itinerate up and down the Annapolis Valley from Windsor to Annapolis throughout June and July 1785. Then in late July he visited Liverpool and, a month later, made his way to the Loyalist centre of Shelburne. Garrettson noted in his journal:

Our dear Master began to carry on a blessed work; but the devil and his children were angry. They frequently stoned the house; and one night a company came out, and strove (as it stood by the brow of a hill on pillars) to shove it down – whilst I was preaching to near four hundred people by candlelight, they were beating underneath, to get away the pillars. In the midst of my preaching I cried out, *Without are dogs, sorcerers, whore mongers, idolaters, and whoever loveth and maketh a lie.* The company ran off with a hideous yelling, and we were left to worship God peaceably.

Then Garrettson went on:

During my stay in and around Shelburne (which was six weeks) numbers both white and black, were added to the society; and many tested the good word of God, and felt the powers of the world to come.[63]

In the early autumn of 1785, Garrettson returned to Halifax to take charge of the extensive Halifax circuit, which required regular visits to Windsor, Cornwallis, and Horton. In the spring of 1786, Garrettson once again visited Liverpool where he observed to John Wesley that though "Alline's small party oppose us warmly the greater part of the town attend our ministry, and the first people have joined our society."[64] After this success Garrettson made his way to the Loyalist centre Shelburne, then a town in serious decline, and on to Barrington. The people of Barrington, having been warned by Thomas Handley Chipman, the New-Light and Baptist minister located at Granville, that Garrettson was "a dangerous 'Arminian'," were initially unresponsive. Despite Chipman's warning, however, hundreds turned out to listen to the visiting Methodist from Maryland. "Between two and three hundred were awakened in a greater or less degree," reported a delighted Garrettson and "their shyness and prejudices were all removed."[65]

Scores of people in settlements along the South Shore, in places like Barrington and Cape Negro, were converted. And because of what Garrettson called "this visitation of the Spirit," Methodist churches were organized on what was then called the "Arminian plan."[66] The stress placed on "free grace"; the possibility of the "second blessing," the Methodist experience of sanctification; and the warm fellowship of the "class meeting" – all appealed to those Nova Scotians who wanted Alline's evangelical Christianity but not the excesses of some of his followers. Garrettson described an especially memorable Sunday during his Barrington sojourn in the following manner:

This morning my mind was amazingly distressed. I was afraid the Lord had not called me to this town. I mourned in secret, and entreated the Lord to make it manifest that he had sent me to this place, by a display of his convincing power among the people. The hour came, and I repaired to the meeting-house; none were present but my pilot (and he was greatly shaken, and in doubt which way to go) and two others. My distress of mind was to be sensibly felt. I withdrew to a little wood, a quarter of a mile from the meeting-house and entreated the Lord, if he required me to preach in the place, to send out the people and bless his word. As I was again ascending the hill toward the meeting-house, resolving within myself: that if the people did not attend, and if the word was not blest, I would leave the town, and conclude that I was not called thereto. But I saw the people coming from every part of the town, and in a short time, we had a large gathering, and immediately the cloud broke from my mind, and with a glad heart I ascended the pulpit stairs; and the word of the Lord seemed all open to me. I preached, and the flame ran through the assembly: in the afternoon I preached again, with the same freedom. Among two or three hundred people it appeared as though there were but few present, but in a greater or less degree felt the flame. After meeting was ended, they came around me on every hand in tears; and I suppose I had invitations to more than twenty houses.[67]

In the autumn of 1786 Garrettson returned to Halifax. During the following winter months he was largely responsible for coaxing into existence yet another revival, in Horton and Cornwallis. " I have had a blessed winter among them," Garrettson observed to John Wesley on 10 March 1787. "If the work continues much longer as it has done, the greater part of the people will be brought in." In Horton, especially, there had "been a divine display; many convinced and converted to God." Garrettson also noted that: "God is carrying on his work in a glorious manner in Barrington; the people flock from every quarter to hear the word: many have been convinced, and about fourteen have been set at liberty, some of whom were famous for all manner of wickedness. The fields here seem white for harvest."[68] Despite Nova Soctia's "white fields" all "ready for harvest," Garrettson left the colony one month later for the United States. He had "received a letter from Dr. Coke [who would succeed Wesley] in which I was requested to attend the Baltimore Conference ... It was with reluctance I came to this country," he observed in April 1787, "but I now feel a willingness to labour and suffer in the cause of God, among this people."[69] Garrettson, however, would never return to Nova Scotia – not only because of his strong sense of being and wanting to remain an American, especially once he had returned to his homeland, but also because, as he once cogently put it, "I was not clear that I had a call to leave the United States."[70]

Garrettson sailed from Nova Scotia on 10 April 1787. Despite the fact he had spent little more than two years in the Maritimes, he had a significant influence on both the Methodist and Baptist causes in the region, right into the twentieth century. As R.D. Simpson so aptly observed in 1984, "Garrettson's impact upon Nova Scotia was almost equal to that of Wesley in Great Britain and Asbury in the United States."[71]

Garrettson and Alline, so alike yet so different, were an extraordinary team. The religious landscape of the Maritimes was permanently altered because of the charismatic preaching of these two American-born evangelists.

I have discussed the careers of Alline and Garrettson in some detail because these men were religious giants. They certainly established the revivalistic and evangelical paradigm for the Maritime region. Before I began reexamining the life of Alline in the late 1970s, and before I began studying Freeborn Garrettson's Nova Scotia career in the early 1980s, however, I had been attracted to the work of Anthony Wallace.

At the core of the Wallace thesis is an emphasis on what the sociologist Seymour M. Lipset has referred to as the need for people under stress to find "a dynamic equilibrium" between what has been referred to as "autonomous action and changing experiences."[72] Consequently, for Wallace and his disciples, "A religious revival or a great awakening begins when accumulated pressures for change produce such acute personal and social stress that the whole culture must break the crust of custom, crash through the blocks in the mazeways, and find new socially structured avenues along which the members of the society may pursue their course in mutual harmony with one another."[73] And for Wallace the charismatic "prophet" leads the way towards "dynamic equilibrium." He or she

reveals (as God's chosen messenger) this new way to his fellow men. Gradually he develops a band of disciples or followers, whom he appoints (or anoints) and they fan out through the social system to proselytize for the new religious order. Among the precepts they inculcate are not only theological statements regarding the nature and will of God and how he is to be worshipped but also (more or less explicitly) a new set of social norms for individual and group behaviour. Those who come in contact with the prophet or his charismatic disciples are "touched" by the same divine experience, and this validates both the prophet's vision and the new mazeways he inculcates as God's will for his people.[74]

The charisma of the prophet or prophetess and his or her disciples need not be only an extraordinarily powerful "attribute of individual personality or a mystical quality." There is an important social relationship involved in charisma as well.[75] As far as the influential sociologist Peter Worsley is concerned, charisma provides much "more than an abstract ideological rationale." It is, he argues, stretching Wallace a little further: "a legitimization grounded in a relationship of loyalty and identification in which the leader is followed simply because he embodies values in which the followers have an 'interest' ... The followers ... in a dialectical way, create, by selecting them out, the leaders who in turn *command* on the basis of this newly-accorded legitimacy ... He articulates and consolidates their aspirations."[76]

The Wallace revitalization thesis, it should be stressed, was not used simplistically to explain all aspects of the widespread social movement that engulfed Nova Scotia and New Brunswick during the American Revolution. Rather, I found that the insights which Wallace provided, largely from his study *The Death and Rebirth of the Seneca* but also in his seminal article "Revitalization Movements," could be carefully gleaned to throw new light on Henry Alline, his message, and the remarkable impact he had on Nova Scotia and Northern New England. Thus for me Wallace's revitalization thesis was a descriptive device rather than an explanatory one. It provided me with the opportunity to locate my reassessment of Alline within the context of Wallace's influential thesis. In other words, and to be disconcertingly blunt, my *Ravished By The Spirit: Religious Revivals, Baptists and Henry Alline* was an attempt to associate my work closely with that of Wallace and W.G. McLoughlin, the author of *Revivals, Awakenings and Reform*, a historian who was very much influenced by Wallace. This was not, I hoped, an example of guilt by association but rather of augmented relevance and importance by association. I was eager to locate my work on what I considered to be the leading edge of American religious scholarship. Since most Canadian scholars remained uninterested in what I was doing, I looked longingly southward, both for inspiration and recognition. Perhaps this was a mistake, perhaps it was not.

I further strengthened my growing dependence on American ideological constructs by using the work of Victor Turner in much the same way I was using Anthony Wallace's revitalization thesis. Wallace, for me, threw considerable light on Alline and his disciples, as well as on the role they played in triggering scores of revivals in the Maritimes during and after the American Revolution. But as I moved into the post-Alline period, Wallace seemed to become less and less relevant. Looming larger and larger was the question: why were so many ordinary Nova Scotians and New Brunswickers during the first three or four decades of the nineteenth century – the time of the so-called Second Great Awakening – so deeply affected by evangelical religion as it was manifested in the series of intense religious revivals that swept the region? For an answer, I was tempted to appropriate the social control model which Paul Johnson appeared to use so effectively in *A Shopkeeper's Millennium: Society and Revivals in Rochester, New York, 1815-1837*. Yet when I tried to apply this model to Yarmouth, Nova Scotia, in the first decade of the nineteenth century, or to Liverpool, Nova Scotia, at the same time, or to other Maritime communities in the 1820s as they were convulsed by religious revivals, I saw that the model made little sense. There was no evidence that members of a middle- or upperclass in these communities were using religious revivals to protect their increasingly threatened interests. In fact the evidence suggested quite the opposite, that the revivals were viewed by the Maritime élite as being almost revolutionary threats to the *status quo*. These people tended to equate revivalism with American and, later, French republicanism and they did everything in their power to eradicate from the land what they disparagingly referred to as "New Light Fanaticism."[77] Bishop Charles Inglis, of Nova Scotia, had expressed the Maritime establishment view in April 1799: "Fanatics are impatient under civil restraint & run into the democratic system. They are for leveling everything both sacred and civil; & this is peculiarly the case of our New Lights [the disciples of Henry Alline and Freeborn Garrettson] who are, as far as I can learn, Democrats to a man."[78] The Inglis view was to prevail in the Maritime region for much of the pre-Confederation period.

If the Johnston social control model was, as it has been recently argued and as I had found, totally "obsolete,"[79] then it seemed reasonable for me to accept passively, as a given, the anticipated biting critique of my neo-Marxist scholar friends and to disregard it to look seriously at Victor Turner instead. This I did during my 1982/3 sabbatical at Harvard University. I tried to read all that I could find written by Turner and I religiously attended one of his public lectures at Harvard.

I began to realize that Turner, especially in *The Ritual Process: Structure and Anti-Structure*, had provided me with yet another possible explanatory and descriptive framework in which I could locate the popular evangelical response to revivals and revivalists in the Maritimes in the early nineteenth century. What I had found lacking in Wallace and McLoughlin I discovered, often in opaque literary form, in Turner.

Through the prism provided by *The Ritual Process* I began to see late eighteenth and early nineteenth century revivals, in particular, as special rituals whereby, as Turner had brilliantly suggested, "well-bonded" human beings had created "by structural means" what he has called the "classificatory nets" for their "routinized spheres of action." And by "verbal and non-verbal means" religious revivals became the instrument whereby large numbers of Maritimers and Canadians were able to break away from their "innumerable constraints and boundaries" and capture what Turner has called the "floating world" of self-discovery, inner freedom, and actualization.

Everyone, according to Turner, alternates between "fixed" and "floating" worlds. They oscillate, in other words, between, on the one hand, preoccupation with order and constraint and, on the other hand, a search for novelty and freedom. Thus, for thousands of Maritimers, revivals were the occasion to experience first-hand and with intensity what has been termed an "anti-structural liminality." The religious revival thus became the actual social means whereby all sorts of complex and hitherto internalized and sublimated desires, dreams, hopes, and aspirations became legitimized. Traditional behaviour and values were often openly challenged; and the "anti-structural liminality" of the revival ritual helped to give shape and form, however transitory, to a deeply satisfying "tender, silent, cognizant mutality." Seemingly aberrant behaviour, such as women and children exhorting publicly that their husbands and fathers needed to be converted, became "rituals of status reversal." "Cognitively," as Turner points out, "nothing underlines regularity as well as absurdity or paradox" and "emotionally nothing satisfies as much as extravagant or temporarily permitted illicit behaviour." Grown men could weep openly during a revival; this was widely perceived as a sign of grace and not a sign of weakness. Married women could publicly chastise their husbands during the revival; this abandoning of deference was accepted as the work of the Holy Spirit, as was the often intense criticism by children of their unChristian and worldly parents.

According to Turner, there is in the ritual process an intensely satisfying and intensely pleasurable feeling of fellowship – as the "ecstasy of spontaneous communitas" overwhelms everyone involved, directly or indirectly, in the ritual process in general and the revival in particular. Spontaneous communitas produced by rituals like revivals had something almost "'magical' about it." Almost despite themselves people shared, for what seemed eternity but was only a fragile moment, a "feeling of endless power." And this feeling which I saw expressed in numerous Maritime revivals is both exhilarating and frightening. When applied specifically to revivals this bonding – this "mystery of intimacy" – drew men, women, and children towards one another, triggering a Christian love that challenged what seemed to be a selfish, circumscribed, almost worldly, fidelity. People saw Christ in their friends and their neighbours and they wanted ever so desperately to love their friends as they loved their Christ. Some apparently did, or so they wrote; their joy must have been intense as they looked at the world from the peak of religious ecstasy. Then they realized, often to their bitter sorrow, that spontaneous communitas was only a "phase, a moment, not a permanent condition" as the reality of "distancing and of tradition" regained firm control in the community. But people had behaved differently during the revival and some people had been permanently changed. Some would never replicate their peak religious experience. Others would, during religious revivals that became the means whereby their Christian faith was frequently both renewed and revitalized.[80]

The ecstasy of spontaneous communitas and the mystery of intimacy were crucially important and common themes I had perceived in the series of late eighteenth- and early nineteenth-century revivals I examined in some detail in the early 1980s. Turner's *Ritual Process* gave me the academic courage to pursue my work on Maritime revivals from the bottom up, rather than from the top down, and from inside, rather than from outside. Or at least I wanted to move in these directions despite the fact that I often lacked what one reviewer of *Ravished By The Spirit* correctly referred to as the necessary demographic and statistical data to support my generalizations. But, unfortunately, the data for what he called "thick history"[81] was not readily available. However, as one moved into the nineteenth century, more and more material surfaced which could be used to reconstruct revivals from the bottom up and from inside out.

My borrowings from Wallace and Turner certainly promised me a degree of academic respectability. More than that, these men gave me implicit encouragement at a time when I had serious reservations about being too sympathetic to or showing too much empathy for the Canadian evangelical tradition. I had for a variety of reasons felt a deep inner need during 1982 and 1983, in particular, to re-examine the Nova Scotia revivalist tradition in general and Henry Alline in particular. But I had not wanted to jettison whatever academic reputation I had by being too closely associated with revivals and revivalists, even those of the distant Canadian past. I understood only too well from my vantage-point at Queen's University the largely secular bias of so much contemporary Canadian historical writing and I did not want to be pushed even further to the outer margins of the profession. My work on the Maritimes had already distanced me to a certain degree, since for so many Canadian historians Maritime historians are of peripheral importance. And underscoring for many the marginality of my work was the fact that so much of it dealt with the seventeenth and eighteenth centuries – the so-called Dark Ages of Canadian History. Writing about revivals and revivalists would, I was certain, push me even further to the outskirts. But it became clear to me as early as October 1981, when I was asked by Acadia Divinity College to give the 1983 Hayward Lectures, that I had little to lose in pursuing this work. There was perhaps even something to gain: I could become involved in the vigourous North American debate about the evangelical tradition. For even though many Canadian scholars were not much interested in my work, some American scholars were. From their reviews, letters, and invitations, I knew that a number of them were taking some of my work on Maritime religion very seriously indeed. I saw this first in Stephen Marini's "New England Folk Religions 1770–1815: The Sectarian Impulse in Revolutionary Society," later published by Harvard University Press under the title *Radical Sects of Revolutionary New England*. Then I saw it in the work of Nathan Natch, a historian at Notre Dame, and Mark Noll, of Wheaton College, Illinois – among others. I was naturally drawn to their intellectual milieu and their attempt to reassess the impact of the evangelical tradition on American religious, social, political, and economic development. I found myself invited to annual seminars at Cape Cod organized by Hatch and Noll, at which certain aspects of the North American evangelical tradition were examined from a variety of different perspectives. At these seminars I met George Marsden, the author of *Fundamentalism and American Culture: The Shaping of Twentieth-Century Evangelicalism 1870–1925*. Widely regarded as a "remarkable accomplishment,"[82] Marsden's volume has been described by Martin Marty of the University of Chicago, and with good reason, as one of the most important books about American religion published in the twentieth century.

What Marsden had done, as far as I was concerned anyway, was to make academically respectable the serious and sympathetic study of American fundamentalism. If Marsden could do this for American fundamentalism – a movement I must confess, I had very little sympathy for – why could I not at least attempt to throw some scholarly light on Canadian revivals and revivalists in the eighteenth and ninteenth centuries – happenings and people I was not necessarily unsympathetic to?

There is a remarkable "afterward" to be found in Marsden's *Fundamentalism*. This afterward, which is permeated by the author's rigorous integrity and scholarly honesty, has been permanently etched into my consciousness. According to Marsden:

It is basic Christian doctrine that there is an awesome distance between God and his creation, and yet that God nevertheless enters human history and acts in actual historical circumstances. The awareness that God acts in history in ways that we can only know in the context of our culturally determined experience should be central to a Christian understanding of history. Yet the Christian must not lose sight of the premise that, just as in the Incarnation, Christ's humanity does not compromise his divinity so the reality of God's other work in history, going well beyond what we might explain as natural phenomena, is not compromised by the fact that it is culturally defined.

Then Marsden goes on:

The history of Christianity reveals a perplexing mixture of divine and human factors. As Richard Lovelace has said, this history, when viewed without a proper awareness of the spiritual forces involved, "is as confusing as a football game in which half the players are invisible." The present work, an analysis of cultural influences on religious belief, is a study of things visible. As such it must necessarily reflect more than a little sympathy with the modern mode of explanation in terms of natural historical causation. Yet it would be a mistake to assume that such sympathy is incompatible with, or even antagonistic to, a view of history in which God as revealed in Scripture is the dominant force, and in which other unseen spiritual forces are contending. I find that a Christian view of history is clarified if one considers reality as more or less like the world portrayed in the works of J.R.R. Tolkien. We live in the midst of contests between great and mysterious spiritual forces, which we understand only imperfectly and whose true dimensions we only occasionally glimpse. Yet, frail as we are, we do play a role in this history, on the side either of the powers of light or of the powers of darkness. It is crucially important then, that, by God's grace, we keep our wits about us and discern the vast difference between the real forces for good and the powers of darkness disguised as angels of light.[83]

As far as Marsden is concerned, the "Christian historian," though attached to certain theological criteria, may nevertheless "refrain from explicit judgments on what is properly Christian" while at the same time concentrating "on observable cultural forces ... By identifying these forces, [he or she] provides material which individuals of various theological persuasions may use to help distinguish God's genuine work from practices that have no greater authority than the customs or ways of thinking of a particular time and place."[84]

Though I may have some serious intellectual reservations about the Lovelace-Tolkien-Marsden view of cosmic reality, I consider it as plausible an explanatory device for historical development and change as many other theories that are widely used and academically popular. Though this view may not influence directly my own historical approach, it has compelled me to look at other approaches to the evangelical tradition in a far more sympathetic manner. If neo-Marxists can write neo-Marxist history, why should not evangelical Christian historians – like Marsden – write from an evangelical Christian perspective? Furthermore, why should not a scholar knowledgeable and at least sympathetic to the evangelical tradition today write about the evangelical tradition of yesterday? There is no reason for me to make pious and "explicit judgments on what is properly Christian." It is my hope, as it is Marsden's, that by identifying some of "these observable cultural forces" I will help people whose theological views are quite different from mine to "distinguish God's genuine work from practices that have no greater authority than the customs or ways of thinking of a particular time and place." At one time such an approach would have been anathema to me. Today it is not, largely because of the indirect and direct influence of American scholars such as George Marsden.

Even a superficial reading of my work of the past decade will reveal the influence of Wallace, Turner, and Marsden. Sometimes Wallace's influence seems to be of primary importance, and so explicit, and sometimes Turner's. And then there is George Marsden's implicit influence; almost everywhere and nowhere is it recognized explicitly. But despite what to some might be my growing dependence on Wallace and Turner I hope that I have not been shackled or in any way intellectually stultified by their work. I have attempted to use their insights with care, usually for descriptive rather than analytical purposes. I have mixed their often brilliant themes of religious change together and added some of my own interpretations to produce, I hope, a novel way of looking at revivals and revivalists. In all of the rather different revivals I have looked at, whether they occurred in Nova Scotia or what is now Ontario, or whether they took place in the 1770s, 1850s or, 1920s, I have emphasized the crucial role played by charismatic preachers. They are people who are widely perceived as having simple and direct answers for often complex personal and theological problems. They have their greatest impact when they direct people who are experiencing serious problems with personal and group relationships to a personal relationship to Jesus Christ – the perceived Son of God. This personal relationship with Christ, which is often triggered by a traumatic conversion experience, seems to solve, at least for a while, all problems arising from disintegrating and disintegrated relationships. The ecstasy of conversion supplemented by Christian love and the sense of community provided by the revivals creates an atmosphere for further conversions. Despite the real trauma of conversion and of revivals, there are in the Maritime context, at least, few manifestations of emotional excess.

Often there are tears and sobbing, and sometimes people are "struck by the Spirit," but in all the revivals I have examined in the three Maritime provinces I have yet to come across one which can be characterized as being wild and frenzied. This is not to suggest that there were not any in what is now Canada. We know that there were "barking" and "babbling in tongues," as well as powerful physical convulsions, the so-called jerks and works, in the McDonaldite revivals on Prince Edward Island in the nineteenth century.[85] There were similar occurrences in many Methodist camp meetings in what is now Ontario and Quebec in the early decades of the nineteenth century. Yet the evidence is overwhelming, when all of the Maritime revivals from the 1770s to the 1920s are taken into account, that they were remarkably well-ordered. It was as though the Canadian and the Maritime obsession with "peace, order, and good government" also shaped the region's revivalist tradition.

The Alline-Garrettson revivalist tradition, within the context of the nineteenth century and the early decades of the twentieth century, significantly shaped Maritime Protestant religious culture and Maritime historical development, even though we know so little about this shaping process. There are at least four major ways in which Maritime revivalism may have substantially impinged upon the Maritime experience.

First, there are the raw, denominational numbers. By the late nineteenth century, for example, one in four New Brunswickers was a Baptist, and one in five Nova Scotians, but only one in twenty Islanders; about one in ten persons was a Methodist in New Brunswick and Nova Scotia combined and one in eight on Prince Edward Island.

Second, there was an important, almost contradictory impact on the region's political culture. On the one hand, in the revivalistic tradition there was a tremendous stress placed on individual conversion – upon the individual's special and continuing personal relationship with Christ and with eternal varieties rather than with mundane, here and now, largely ephemeral, societal problems. Because of this some historians have understandably concluded that Maritime revivalism strengthened considerably the "conservative political culture of the region." "The political culture of the region," it has been argued as late as December 1987, "had congealed by the 1850s into something 'fundamentally conservative' and traditional and this process of congealment owed a great deal to the power of Evangelical religion in this region."[86] It would be wrong, however, to stop here and to forget "the other hand" – the communitarian side of the evangelical message. Alline, Garrettson, and their scores of nineteenth-century disciples were also very concerned about transforming society – about making it more Christ-like. Converted individuals, they contended, would try nobly to transform society into the "New Jerusalem." Alline and Garrettson were certainly not preoccupied with the imminent and apocalyptic end of the world. In fact, well on into the twentieth century, both of these charismatic preachers and most of their followers tended to equate true conversion on this earth with an immediate entry into heaven and eternal bliss. For Alline and others, "heaven on earth" was something they "blissfully" experienced. For Alline, in particular, there was no such thing as linear history. Since God lived in what he often referred to as the *"One Eternal Now,"* surely, the Falmouth preacher argued, the truly redeemed of the Lord "must inhabit the same" at precisely the moment he or she reached out to the Almighty since "the work of conversion is instantaneous."[87] According to Alline, for all those who had experienced the New Birth, there was indeed no sense of "Time, and Space, and Successive Periods." "Salvation and Damnation," Alline stressed,

originate here at your own Door; for with God there never was any Thing, as before or after, Millions of Ages, before time began, and as many more, after Time is at a Period, being the same very instant; consider neither Time past nor Time to come, but one Eternal Now; consider that with God there is neither Succession nor Progress; but that with Him the Moment He said let us make Man, and the Sound of his last Trumpet, is the very same instant, and your Death as much first as your Birth ... with God all things are NOW ... as the Center of a Ring, which is as near the one side as the other.[88]

Regeneration was thus seen by Alline as the mystical process which destroyed artificial time and space and, astonishingly, transformed for each individual the mundane, what Alline described as the world of "Turnips, Cabbages and Potatoes" into the cosmic and heavenly – "the Eternity you once, were, and knew."[89]

While on this earth, Alline's followers were urged to labour diligently "for the promotion of religion, the advancing of Christ's kingdom, as far as the influence of your several stations and capacities in life may extend."[90] Even though he instructed his followers to abandon "their earthly joys, pleasures, and recreations"[91] and to reject "the carnal world and pleasures of Egypt,"[92] they were expected to use their Christian zeal not only to witness to others but also to try to transform Nova Scotia society. It was Alline's contention that regeneration "will naturally produce a christian deportment externally as fire will produce light."[93] He urged the leaders of Nova Scotia society, "the capital men" and the "Counsellors," to "be a Terror to evil doers."[94] "O embrace the unspeakable privilege," Alline declared, "and let me intreat you to adorn your station by the grace of God, and live as lights in the world, and for the Lord's sake, your own souls sake, and the sake of others around you arise up and witness for God, and let all your deportment espouse the redeemers cause, and the welfare of souls."[95] The "welfare of souls," for Alline, meant being lovingly concerned about "ye Poor, ye blind, ye sick, ye sore, ye lame, and miserable."[96] This is what Alline meant when he preached about "advancing ... Christ's kingdom as far as the influence of your several stations and capacities in life may extend."[97]

Charles Finney's postmillennial optimism was apparently shared by most Maritime Baptists and Methodists in the nineteenth and early twentieth centuries. In 1846, for example, Finney, the great American evangelist declared:

Now the great business of the church is to reform the world – to put away every kind of sin. The church was originally organized to be a body of reformers. The very profession of Christianity implies the profession and virtually an oath to do all that can be done for the reformation of the world. The Christian church was designed to make aggressive movements in every direction – to lift up her voice and put forth her energies in high and low places – to reform individuals, communities and governments, and never rest until the Kingdom and the greatness of the Kingdom under the whole heaven shall be given to the saints of the Most High God – until every form of iniquity shall be driven from the earth.[98]

Should one be surprised therefore to discover that in 1921 the Maritime United Baptist Convention, but not the Baptist Convention of Ontario and Quebec, adopted the following nineteen-point progressive, social gospel "platform":

1   Every child has the right to be well born, well nourished, and well protected.
2   Every child has the right to play and be a child.
3   Every child is entitled to such an education as shall fit it for life and usefulness.
4   Every life is entitled to a sanitary home, pure air, and pure water.
5   Every life is entitled to such conditions as shall enable it to grow up tall and straight and pure.
6   Every life is entitled to a place in society, a good opportunity in life and a fair equity in the common heritage.
7   The resources of the earth being the heritage of the people, should not be monopolized by the few to the disadvantage of the many.
8   The stewardship of property requires that all property held be supervised, moralized and spiritualized.
9   Work should be done under proper conditions with respect to hours, wages, health, management and morals.
10 Every worker should have one day's rest in seven and reasonable time for recreation and family life.
11 Women who toil should have equal pay with men for equal work.
12 Widowed mothers with dependent children should be relieved from the necessity of exhausting toil.
13 Employers and employees are partners in industry and should be partners in the enterprise.

14   Suitable provision should be made for old age workers and for those incapacitated by injury and sickness.
15   Income received and benefits enjoyed should hold a direct relation to service rendered.
16   The State which punishes vice should remove the causes which make [people] more vicious.
17   The bond of brotherhood is the final and fundamental fact and men are called to organize all life, ecclesiastical, civic, social, industrial, on the basis of brotherhood.
18   The help should be greatest where the need is most.
19   What the few now are, many may become.[99]

As late as 1940, moreover, the Maritime Baptist Convention endorsed the statement "that far reaching changes ... in the political and economic life of the nation ... are coming, and in fact have come which are bound to greatly affect the economic system." "We believe," the social service report went on, "that future movements will be inevitably toward greater governmental and centralized control and regulation. We have faith, however, that there will come a larger and fairer distribution of the national income among all classes."[100] Similar strong progressive social gospel declarations were endorsed by the Maritime conference of the United Church in the late 1920s and 1930s. This Evangelical social-gospel consensus was superbly captured in the Maritime United Baptist Convention declaration of 1936: "It might be said of our Baptist fathers that they brought religion to the towns, villages and settlements of these provinces, for they went everywhere preaching the word. We trust that it will be said for us and our generation, that we kept religion alive in these places, that we nurtured every wholesome social endeavor and that, at all times we have put in the first place, the Kingdom of God and his righteousness."[101]

Third, the revivalist tradition which, in fact, became the Maritime-Baptist-Methodist mainstream – and thus the Protestant mainstream – had always placed greater emphasis on "promoting a good work," or in other words bringing about conversions and revivals, than on theological or doctrinal purity and conformity. From the time of Alline and Garrettson, the evangelical mainstream, especially at the grass-roots level, had been basically syncretic as well as experiential. It was emphatically the religion of an Alline or a Garrettson rather than that of a T.T. Shields (the influential twentieth century Ontario

Baptist fundamentalist). And this experiential, and sometimes mystical, open-minded evangelical theology would characterize the Maritime-Methodist-Baptist religious experience until the late 1930s and even beyond. During the post-WW-II period, however, as the Maritime region was both increasingly Upper Canadianized and Americanized, this unique religious culture – which was crucial to Maritime identity – would be undermined by the corrosive impact of modernity and so-called progress, as well as by the loss of confidence among the people in things uniquely Maritime.

Fourth, it is clear that the Maritime revivalist tradition from the time of Alline placed almost inordinate emphasis on "ordered" revivals. Even the McDonaldite "works" on Prince Edward Island, widely perceived as the notable exception to the Maritime evangelical norm, as David Weale has persuasively argued, were remarkably controlled and almost organized affairs.[102]

As the twentieth century unfolded, the revivalist tradition in the Maritimes lost much of its power and influence. What has been called the evangelical nineteenth century was replaced by the largely secular twentieth century. The number of Baptists and Methodists has fallen significantly: in the early 1980s Baptists made up a little more than 10 per cent of the total Maritime population. The social-gospel tradition has been largely abandoned – especially by the Baptists – and replaced for many by an imported variant of American-fundamentalist neo-conservatism.[103] And, the Allinite-Garrettsonian emphasis on experiential religion and zeal balanced by order has been pushed to the periphery of the religious culture of the region by an increasingly closed-minded theological fundamentalism largely borrowed from the United States and Central Canada. Finally, since there have been so few large-scale community revivals in the twentieth century, there has been no need to discuss the advantages and disadvantages of traditional ordered revivals, as opposed to "frenzied group behaviour."

In the twentieth century much of what would be preached by the new prophets of evangelical consumerism and greed would, in fact, be the antithesis of nineteenth century evangelicalism. And the decline in importance of Canadian and Maritime revivalism may be a significant religious statement. Unable to see anything but the gross hypocrisy of the modern gospel, and revolted by the spiritual hubris of fundamentalism, tens of thousands of Canadians are satisfied with abandoning Christianity altogether. The fastest growing group in Canada in the 1980s continues to be the "one that professes no religion at all." In the Maritimes, as Reginald Bibby has recently argued, there has been an almost desperate attempt by many Protestants in particular to cling to whatever might remain of the crumbling edifice of the nineteenth century evangelical consensus. They thus slide into the twenty-first century looking longingly backwards to a nineteenth century, which, even to the sharp Maritime eye, is becoming dimmer and dimmer. Or is it? Perhaps they are merely resonating with Jacques Ellul's bitter lament "Beyond Jesus, beyond him, there is nothing – nothing but lies."[104]

2 Fundamentalism, Modernism, and the Maritime Baptists in the 1920s and 1930s

Some English-Canadian historians find it embarrassingly difficult to take religion seriously. As they comb the past for relevance and what recently have been called the collective *Habits of the Heart*,[1] they are keen to avoid any confrontation with spiritual and religious realities. Perhaps they are uncomfortable thinking about such issues. Perhaps, because of the older Whig political bias of so much Canadian historical writing and the newer bias of secular social history, they are determined to float in the mainstream of historiography and not be lost in some shallow cul-de-sac. This of course may be regarded, with some justification, as an unfair caricature of the Canadian historical profession. Yet the exaggeration should underscore some of the basic problems confronting those writing religious history in English Canada in the 1980s. When compared with American historiography, it is clear that English-Canadian historians have significantly downplayed the importance of religion as a formative force in Canadian life. Our historical writing, especially that of the post-World-War-II period, reflects the devastating impact of what has been referred to as "that process of separation and individualism that modernity seems to entail."[2]

A sensitive reading of our collective religious past should bring what Stephen Toulmin has called a degree of "cosmic interrelatedness"[3] back to our scholarly investigation. I am, of course, not suggesting that a revived and renewed and American-ized Canadian religious history is the only way to accomplish this end. But, to my mind, it is certainly one viable way. For me, studying and writing history and connecting the past and the present are not as profoundly separate as some might think. If we could, at least,

begin to discuss critically and openly issues of religion, values, community, individualism, and space and time "in ways that did not
disaggregate them into fragments," it might still be possible "for us
to find connections and analogies with the older ways in which
human life was made meaningful."[4] I am not proposing, however,
a return to a neotraditionalism that would suddenly and almost
magically transfer us to a distant past. Rather, as has been recently
argued, a particularly perceptive reading of the past "might lead to
a recovery of a genuine tradition, one that is always self-revising
and in a state of development."[5] It might help us, notably in Canada
and the Western World, to "find again the coherence we have almost
lost."[6]

For me, first-class historical writing and teaching must always try
to link effectively and sensitively the past and the present. Links of
this kind must at least be attempted. Our collective religious experience provides one key link. We owe much of the essential meaning
of our lives to our religious traditions about which, unfortunately,
we now infrequently think. And we face, in my view, the very real
possibility that the further undermining of these traditions "may
eventually deprive us of that meaning altogether."[7] I am, however,
neither a Cassandra nor a Jeremiah – merely a concerned historian
who has only recently recaptured a deep interest in this country's
religious past.

Ironically, within the larger context of the recent historiography
of the Maritime provinces, religious history has not been pushed off
into some dark corner of irrelevance, inconsequence, and scholarly
oblivion. Since the early 1970s at least, the writing of religious history
has become "probably the most active and exciting field of historical
scholarship in the Maritimes today."[8] Post-revolutionary Maritime
history, with its emphasis on the significant influence of the Allinite-
New Light legacy, has now found itself on what is, to some, the
leading edge of the discipline in Canada.[9] A caustic critic might
simply comment that taking into account the sad state of contemporary Canadian religious writing, such a claim is indeed a modest
one. Another might respond that the peripheral nature of so much
Maritime historical writing is merely underscored by the fact that
what is seen as a scholarly cul-de-sac by the Central Canadian
opinion-makers is viewed as the mainstream by scholars in or of the
region.

There is a ring of truth, moreover, to Professor Terrence Murphy's argument that religious developments in the Maritime region in the immediate post-revolutionary period have already received adequate scholarly attention. He correctly urges historians to abandon an obsession with the Revolution and Henry Alline and to examine nineteenth- and twentieth-century religious leaders, movements, and ideology.[10] In fact, apart from Professor Ernie Forbes' fine article dealing with "Prohibition and the Social Gospel in Nova Scotia,"[11] little of real significance has been published about Protestantism in the Maritimes in the twentieth century, although there are a number of very good studies dealing with Roman Catholicism, especially the Antigonish Movement. Thus the twentieth century beckons the historian interested in virtually any aspect of Protestant religious development in the Maritimes. There is no fear of being criticized as a nasty revisionist. There is almost nothing to revise. Instead, there is the opportunity to establish the framework in which others who may follow will, not too reluctantly, locate themselves.

One group of Protestants that merits immediate study would be the Maritime Baptists. In no other part of Canada have Baptists formed such a large proportion of the population or had such a profound influence on the existing popular culture. Yet almost nothing of importance has been written about the twentieth-century Baptist experience in the Maritimes. On Prince Edward Island the Baptist Church was never an important force, but, in 1901, taking Nova Scotia and New Brunswick as a single entity, the Baptists were the largest Protestant denomination in this area. Twenty years later the Baptists in New Brunswick and Nova Scotia were still the largest Protestant denomination. But, in 1931, they were pushed to second place by the United Church and, in 1961, to third by the Anglicans.[12]

During the 1920s and 1930s, almost every Baptist in the Maritimes belonged to the United Baptist Convention of the Maritime provinces. In 1906 the Regular, or Calvinist, Baptists of the region had joined with the Free Baptists, or Arminians, to create the United Baptist Convention. Acadia University in Wolfville was the convention's institution of higher learning, and the administrative arm of the convention was located in Saint John. During the late 1920s, the unity of the convention was increasingly threatened by the rising tide of fundamentalism that was beginning to spread into the region from Central Canada and the United States.

It is noteworthy that the Maritime Baptist Convention was not split in the same way the Central Canadian Baptists or even the Western Canadian Baptists were.[13] A principal actor in the so-called fundamentalist-modernist controversy both in Central Canada and the West was the Reverend Thomas Todhunter Shields – the influential and controversial Baptist fundamentalist leader who was minister of the Jarvis Street Baptist Church in Toronto from 1910 to 1955.[14] There was no Maritime fundamentalist leader whose influence was comparable to that of Shields, but the United Baptist Maritime Convention did experience a less serious challenge to its authority from the Reverend John James Sidey[15], who became the most outspoken critic of the convention leadership. Thus, in the Maritimes in the 1920s and 1930s, Shield's able lieutenant, the Reverend J.J. Sidey, was not able to attract to his separtist, Baptist, and fundamentalist movement an appreciable number of convention Baptists. Why? Why was not Sidey any more successful in his sectarian offensive in the Baptist heartland of Canada – an area significantly influenced by the radical, evangelical–New Light ethos of the late eighteenth and nineteenth centuries? Why was Sidey's schismatic movement relatively weak, especially given that in the post-World-War-I period the Baptist leadership in the convention was moving off in what to many was a liberal direction?[16]

John James Sidey was born in Portsmouth, England, on 28 December 1891. His father, the Reverend Charles J. Sidey, was a Wesleyan Methodist missionary-minister in Newfoundland, where the young John spent some of his early years.[17] Sidey and his mother later returned to England. Sarah Sidey was a pious Methodist, but her marriage was not a happy one and she separated permanently from her husband when she set sail from Newfoundland for Portsmouth. Consequently, it would be his mother, not his father, who would significantly influence Sidey's spiritual and emotional life at its formative stage.

At the age of fourteen, John Sidey was converted and he soon became an active member of the Pembrook Road Methodist Church, serving as a lay preacher. Encouraged by his mother, Sidey became a dentist's apprentice in Portsmouth. Because of financial problems, and the fact that he had injured his right hand and therefore felt his future as a moulder of false teeth was very limited, he decided to emulate his father and become a Methodist missionary to the New World. But when he left Portsmouth for Nova Scotia in the early summer of 1911, the nineteen-year-old Sidey was still uncertain about his future. He was not ordained; he was not an official recruit of a Methodist Missionary Society; and he was not responding to a specific call from a Nova Scotia Methodist Church. Soon after arriving in Halifax, Sidey made his way to his uncle, the Reverend James Heil, a Methodist minister then living in Windsor. In the summer of 1911, despite what he would write in the 1930s and 1940s, Sidey was disoriented and, as one of his most ardent followers has put it, "uncertain of many things."[18] Assisting his uncle obviously did not satisfy the young Sidey who resolved in 1916 to move to the United States to enroll in two Methodist Episcopal institutions in the Chicago area – Northwestern University and Garrett Biblical Institute.

It has been argued that Sidey went to the United States because he had discovered that "the Nova Scotia institutions were becoming infiltrated" with "a humanistic higher criticism."[19] There may, however, have been other reasons for Sidey's decision in 1916 to emigrate to Illinois. He may have been looking for new worlds to conquer – for a greater challenge than that provided by the relative backwater of Windsor. Or it may have been that the young Methodist did not want to fight for the British cause in Europe.

Conscription did not come to Canada until 1917, but Sidey must have felt intense community pressure, especially in 1915 and 1916, to join in the Christian crusade to eradicate the Germanic anti-Christ. Sidey, who was always more inclined to maternal influence than fatherly-like pressure, may also have wanted to be independent of his uncle. He therefore saw in his move to Chicago an opportunity to resolve a number of difficult personal and career problems.

While attending Northwestern and Garrett, Sidey supported himself financially by accepting a student pastorship associated with the Rock River Methodist Episcopal Conference. He served three Methodist congregations: in South Chicago, Calumet Heights, and Langley Avenue. But a year at Northwestern and Garrett with their "modernistic teaching" was more than enough for Sidey, who transferred to Union Theological College, also located in Chicago, in 1917.[20] Union was basically controlled by the Congregationalists, and here Sidey found that his Methodist Arminian views were challenged by a tough-minded Calvinism. While studying at Union, and serving as a student pastor in southern Chicago, Sidey also found time "to take up YMCA work."[21] Near the end of the war Sidey also assisted the senior chaplain at Fort Sheridan as part of his Methodist pastoral work.[22] While serving the Rock River Methodist Episcopal Conference and the American Army, and while still studying at Union Theological College, Sidey decided to work for a Doctor of Divinity degree at Oriental University, located in Washington, DC. After a "seven or eight months" association with Oriental University – only via correspondence – Sidey was awarded the MA and DD degrees in 1921 for a short thesis entitled "Immortality, the Inevitable Result of a Progressive Universe."[23] A short time after Sidey received his DD, Oriental University was declared a fraudulent degree-mill. A court order permanently closed its doors or, more accurately, sealed its mail-box. In 1921 Sidey also received a Bachelor of Theology degree from Union and was ordained a Methodist Episcopal minister.[24]

Three years earlier Sidey had travelled to Nova Scotia to marry Edna Card, a teacher then residing in Hants County. The young couple returned to Chicago where both of them had a great deal of difficulty dealing with urban life and the new ideas that seemed to be bombarding the Methodist Church in the immediate post-war period. Though apparently successful at Fort Sheridan, Sidey experienced the deep despair of doubt, and morbid introspection seemed to immobilize him. Finally, after much spiritual turmoil, and greatly influenced by two female Salvation Army officers, Sidey found peace of mind through jettisoning what he was learning in the classroom and replacing it with a renewed personal relationship with Christ. "It was a terrific battle," he once observed, "to rid myself of the new ideas that had been, by study and by teaching, superimposed upon the experience of my youth."[25]

While still associated with Fort Sheridan, and spurred by a new sense of evangelical zeal, Sidey and his wife became active in the Soul Winner's Gospel Association which had its headquarters in the St Paul Methodist Episcopal Church in Chicago. Using his considerable musical skills, Sidey conducted his first evangelistic crusade for the Soul Winner's Association in June 1920 at Diamond Lake, Illinois. The publicity for the crusade, which he probably prepared, described Sidey as "a man, who, while college trained, has evidently learned to think for himself. Although he has not yet acquired a reputation as a flowery orator, he has the faculty of forcefully presenting ideas that start and keep you thinking. His addresses are sure to be of uncommon interest to all those who enjoy the exercise of thought."[26] The crusade was something of a disaster for Sidey who, because of his lack of success, felt a desperate need for "the baptism of power of the Holy Spirit."[27] Disheartened and disillusioned, Sidey decided to revitalize his faith by attending the Prophetic Bible Conference at Moody Bible Institute in Chicago. While staying at Moody, Sidey discovered the influential premillennial tract, *The Second Coming of Christ*. Almost immediately Sidey and his wife saw their Christian faith in a radically new light.[28] The imminent return of Christ, the rapture, the emphasis upon the dispensational view of the past, the present and future – all now made marvellous sense. According to the premillennial view, the world was becoming increasingly corrupt and the return of Christ was imminent in order to bring the New Testament Dispensation, or age, to its glorious end. Just before His return, however, all true Christians on earth were to be "raptured" – that is removed temporarily from earth – so that they would not have to endure the bloody and cataclysmic final battle of Armageddon. They would return with their Christ to rule the earth, from Jerusalem, for a thousand-year period. Premillennialism obviously provided Sidey with a new sense of purpose and direction in his life. His favourite verse from the Bible – and this tiny portion of the Scriptures which would eventually be chiselled on his gravestone – came from 1 Thessalonians 4.16, "Waiting until the trumpet of the Lord shall sound." Sidey, however, was not satisfied with merely waiting passively for the Lord to return. He was determined to help prepare the way for Christ's return by preaching the gospel with zeal and conviction; moreover, he desperately wanted to ensure that as many people as possible were, in fact, raptured before the terrible bloody battle of Armageddon.

In late 1920 and early 1921, a revitalized Sidey continued his work with the Soul Winner's Association of Illinois. His publicity brochure now had a somewhat different emphasis:

Impressed by the vital need of spiritual life in the individuals who compose our civilization in this age, he with others, has decided to spend his life at the call of the Holy Spirit, in this tremendous field of evangelization. Mr. Sidey brings to the work a modern point of appeal of the Bible. The challenge "Back to the Bible" is the clarion call of his message. He believes in conversion, real regeneration, not hand-shaking or card-signing; but definite inquiry work followed by the witness of the Holy Spirit. On the other hand, the approach to all this is modern, not fanatical or highly emotional; simply an emphasis upon the Biblical spiritual realities as they have been shown to identify themselves with human nature.[29]

In a period of a few months, Sidey's essential message for the Soul Winner's Association had undergone a fundamental change. There was now a concern about "conversion" and not about "ideas"; there was a new emphasis upon "back to the Bible" and the "witness of the Holy Spirit" rather than "the exercise of thought." Sidey had, in a sense, become a conservative evangelical; he was not yet, the evidence suggests, a fundamentalist. What seemed to separate these two positions was a certain degree of "violence in thought and language" which characterized the fundamentalist mind but not the conservative evangelical.[30] In other words, the former viewed God as a close-minded judge while the latter saw the Almighty as a loving parent. Moreover, for the fundamentalist, confrontation was to be preferred to any form of evangelical accommodation with modernity. By late 1920, however, Sidey was certainly moving quickly in the fundamentalist direction – towards and beyond Moody Bible Institute and light years away from the University of Chicago Divinity School. The latter institution, for Sidey and his Chicago friends, had become the bastion of all the insidious and evil forces of modernism and liberalism then spreading across North America.

Despite the fact that she had two small children to care for, Edna Sidey played a key role in her husband's two Soul Winner's evangelistic campaigns. A vigorous and dynamic woman – intelligent, shrewd, and persuasive – she did not enjoy living in the United States and was keen to return to her beloved Nova Scotia. When her husband's academic work had finally been completed at Union in 1921, and after his ordination, she persuaded him to return to her home in Burlington on the Avon River in Hants County. Soon after, Sidey was baptized by immersion by the Reverend Neil Herman, minister of the Emmanuel Baptist Church in Truro; Herman was a leading Nova Scotia fundamentalist whom Sidey had met in 1916 while spending a summer at Brunswick Street Methodist Church in Truro.

In 1921 Sidey showed little interest in finding a pastorate in a Methodist Church. Instead he resolved to introduce into his adopted province the evangelistic approach he had learned with the Illinois Soul Winner's. His mission was to bring the gospel of Christ to the isolated backwaters of Nova Scotia. His Soul Winner's Association of Nova Scotia became an official branch of the Soul Winner's Association of Chicago.[31] At its first convention held at Cambridge, Hants County, on 1 July 1922, a program was adopted which stressed that the central thrust of the organization was "soul winning" in the rural, largely unchurched areas of the province. It was explicitly stated that the new group was interdenominational and a faith mission – that is, all financial support would come from concerned supporters – and that all of Sidey's followers were to be completely dependent upon the "outpouring of the Holy Spirit" and were not to forsake the "kindred fellowship with other Christians."[32] Sidey organized a small team of dedicated workers and, by the spring and summer of 1922, he saw scores of people, especially in Hants County, converted to his brand of evangelical Christianity. In late 1922 and 1923, Sidey's "Evangelistic band" travelled to Hammonds Plains, near Halifax, and then to the Eastern Shore and Guysborough County.[33] In the Jeddore area, Sidey's team worked very closely with local Baptists. One of the Eastern Shore residents wrote to Sidey on 22 January 1923 that "The work is still growing. Most every person you meet now has something to say about the goodness of God. The men who have gone away to the woods send us beautiful letters telling us how God stands by them in their temptations."[34] On 6 June 1923, it was reported from Jeddore that the revival fires were still burning: "I was down for a month [from Lunenburg] and it was to me the happiest month I have ever spent in my life. I really felt sorry when I had to leave them ... I said to Mother when I went home that it seemed everybody was better looking. Mother said, 'That's happiness,' and I thank God that through Mr. Sidey and his workers that this change has come."[35]

The 1922–23 Eastern Shore revival, which eventually spread into Guysborough County, was the means whereby hundreds of residents of a string of isolated settlements stretching from East Jeddore to Canso experienced the intensely satisfying and intensely pleasurable feeling of Christian fellowship as the "ecstasy of spontaneous communitas"[36] almost overwhelmed them. In Guysborough County in 1923 and 1924, Sidey received enthusiastic support from the Reverend E.W. Forbes, an influential Methodist minister, who would remain close to Sidey throughout the 1920s and 1930s. During the 1923–24 Guysborough County campaign, Sidey "preached 105 sermons (one every night) without a break and never preached the same sermon twice."[37] Yet despite the spiritual revivals he and his team had helped coax into existence, by late 1924 and early 1925 Sidey had become rather disillusioned with the work of the Nova Scotia Soul Winner's Association. Even the publishing of his own monthly newsletter *The Challenge*, which began in 1923, did not dispel Sidey's gnawing doubts about his evangelistic work. Sidey and his team realized that it was one thing to help people experience the New Birth. Hundreds of Nova Scotians and other Maritimers had been converted in the 1922–24 period through the ministry of the Nova Scotia Soul Winner's Association. Yet, once the team left the community and the revival ended, the new converts often found themselves without adequate spiritual nurturing or bitterly divided over which church in the community was the true instrument of the Almighty. A disheartened and disillusioned Sidey observed, "My experience has taught me that, while God has given some pastors a greater gift as evangelists than others, yet, this office would be exercised as among brethren within the framework of the church or denomination to which such men adhere."[38]

After sacrificing four years of his life for the Nova Scotia Soul Winner's Association, Sidey had come to the conclusion that his itinerating evangelistic work may have created more problems than it had resolved and he felt that the time was propitious for him to pastor a single church. He and his wife desired the stability, the regular income, and the peace of mind that they hoped might come from a settled ministry. Preaching 105 different sermons on 105 consecutive days was not something a normal father with a wife and two young children would want to do for the rest of his life. As he entered his mid-30s, J.J. Sidey obviously needed a major change of pace; he needed a church to pastor. But as he looked at his ministerial options in Nova Scotia, he saw few doors open to him. He could neither return to the church of his father nor to the church in which he had been ordained, since both had become part of the United Church of Canada in 1925 and Sidey was opposed to that church because its theology was too modern and its leadership too liberal. Presbyterians opposed to Union had no desire to have him, nor did the Anglicans. But some of Sidey's most ardent supporters in the Soul Winner's Association were Maritime Baptists, and the Reverend Neil Herman, who had baptized him, urged him to join the Maritime Baptist Convention. The Reverend T.T. Shields, whom Sidey had first met in Halifax in 1924, supported the pro-Baptist argument put forward by his friend Herman.

Since Sidey had also conducted evangelistic campaigns in Prince Edward Island in 1923 and 1924, and had been particularly successful in the Bedeque area, it should not be surprising that in 1925 the Central Bedeque United Baptist Church asked him to be their temporary supply minister. No other Baptist church in the Maritimes indicated any interest in issuing a call to Sidey, an ordained Episcopal Methodist minister who had had no previous official contact with the Maritime United Baptist Convention. He would therefore have to be satisfied with being a temporary supply minister in a tiny, peripheral convention church. He obviously had to start somewhere.

Sidey's stayed in Bedeque less than five years, but this period helped to transform him into a committed fundamentalist. Fundamentalism's militant and extreme "opposition to modernism, both as a theology and a cultural secularity, distinguished it from earlier evangelical traditions."[39] As Ernest R. Sandeen[40] and George S. Marsden[41] have argued, fundamentalism in the early twentieth century in North America stressed the importance of certain distinctive beliefs – notably premillennialism and the verbal inerrancy of the Bible, as well as the revivalistic tradition of Dwight L. Moody, the great nineteenth-century American evangelist. In addition, its belief core included a largely traditional Calvinist theology and an emphasis on the substitutionary atonement theory – that Christ had died in the place of all truly redeemed sinners – and also that the true church consisted only of those who had been genuinely converted. For Sidey, the inerrancy of the Scriptures, substitutionary atonement, and premillenialism would be the most important fundamentalist tenets.

While at Bedeque, Sidey became very closely associated with the controversial Reverend John Bolton Daggett, minister at the nearby Tryon United Baptist Church, who was to be Sidey's confidant, aide, and intimate friend until Daggett's death in 1939. A native of Grand Manan Island, Daggett was educated at Colby College, Maine, and was ordained in 1894 as a Free Baptist minister. He played a key role in pushing the somewhat reluctant Free Baptists into union in 1906 with the much larger Regular or Calvinist Maritime Baptist Association. In 1911 he left the United Baptist ministry to become a deputy minister in the New Brunswick Department of Agriculture and served in this capacity until 1917 when he was implicated in the Patriotic Potato Scandal. It was charged that Daggett had not only been the conduit for transferring large sums of money into and out the hands of Conservative party supporters but also that he had lied during the McQueen Commission hearings held in 1918.[42] Driven from the Department of Agriculture, Daggett served as pastor of the Marysville, New Brunswick, United Baptist Church until being called to the Tryon, PEI, United Baptist Church. He ministered there until 1926 when he moved to the Kingston, Nova Scotia, United Baptist pastorate.

Sidey and Daggett were a remarkable team. Though in many respects very different men, their strengths complemented one another. Sidey was tall and robust, full of vigour, and seldom sick. His penetrating grey-blue eyes were often full of fun, and he loved to laugh. Daggett, on the other hand, was sickly, small in stature, and very serious. Unlike Sidey, who carefully hid his emotions from public view, Daggett was a feisty, peppery individual whose quick temper often manifested itself in cutting remarks. He was a battler by nature and, like many others who have also suffered from tuberculosis, he was mercurial, almost manic-depressive. When Daggett lived near him, Sidey was far more aggressive and closed-minded. Daggett helped greatly in making Sidey "the combatant."[43]

Even before Sidey had had time to settle into his new Bedeque charge, he found himself a principal actor in the creation of the Maritime Christian Fundamentalist Association. All Maritimers, and not just Baptists, interested in battling against modernism were invited to a special conference held in Truro in August 1925. The Truro Fundamentalist Conference was hosted by the Immanuel United Baptist Church, and the guest speaker was T.T. Shields, the so-called Spurgeon of Canada and, in the 1920s, Canada's leading fundamentalist. He had already helped to split the Ontario and Quebec Baptist Convention into two warring factions – a split that would be formalized a few years later. At the conference the earlier friendship between Shields and Sidey "was further strengthened" as the former "was used to groom God's man for His job in the Maritimes."[44] Moreover, much to the satisfaction of Shields, a key resolution was adopted that "this meeting having a clear understanding of the issues involved, and realizing that the fundamentals of the gospel are in danger of being obscured in these days, through the widespread acceptance of modern ideas of the Bible, does hereby register its protest, and propose that an organization for the purpose of spreading information as to the real issues involved be formed and shall be known as *The Maritime Christian Fundamentalist Association*."[45] Daggett was elected the interim president of the new association and Sidey, the interim secretary.

The two Island ministers, spurred on by Shields, organized a special conference on Christian fundamentals at Tryon United Baptist Church, from 3-5 November 1925. It was hoped that the conference would attract interested fundamentalists from a wide spectrum of Maritime churches. The main speaker was the Reverend Edward Morris, Rector of St Matthias Anglican Church, Halifax, and a committed premillenialist. A graduate of Wycliffe College in the University of Toronto, Morris had become the Maritime spokesman of the premillennial point of view.[46] Morris did not, however, succeed in breathing much life into the Maritime Christian Fundamentalist Association, which was moribund by January 1926. It is hard to see how the Fundamentalist Association had hoped to expand from its tiny Baptist base in Prince Edward Island. It needed leadership and support from the New Brunswick and Nova Scotia Baptist mainstream, as well as from key sectors of the United Church, the Presbyterian Church, and the Anglicans. In 1925 the United Church had serious organizational problems to worry about, and those Presbyterians who had refused to become part of the United Church were preoccupied with denominational survival. There were only a few evangelical Anglicans, and they were not eager to join an organization dominated by premillennialists and what they must have regarded as bush-league Baptists. Most clergy in the Maritime United Baptist Convention saw no need for such an organization. Their denomination was already sympathetic to certain key elements of the fundamentalist cause; and some of them must have had serious reservations about the leadership of Sidey and Daggett, one an outsider and the other a person with an unsavoury reputation.

The sudden collapse of the Maritime Christian Fundamentalist Association meant that Sidey had more time and energy to devote his Bedeque church and to the Maritime United Baptist Convention. In 1926 Sidey officially became a Baptist by becoming a member of the Central Bedeque United Baptist Church. The following year his church asked the Maritime United Baptist Convention Examining Council for Ordination that "their Pastor Rev. J.J. Sidey, formerly a regularly ordained minister of the Methodist Episcopal body, but now a member of the Bedeque Church, be registered as a regularly ordained Baptist Minister." Together with a former Seventh Day Adventist minister, Sidey was examined by the council for ordination. After hearing "a frank statement" of his "doctrinal views," the council resolved that Sidey's name "be added to our official list."[47] He was listed "Sidey, J.J., MA DD Central Bedeque, 1927."[48]

Sidey loved to write, direct, and produce ambitious religious pageants and he tried to use these pageants to consolidate his position in the convention. His first production, written in 1926, *The Victory of the Gospel*, was based upon the "Wandering Jew" theme. In his foreword Sidey described the essential story. The "Wandering Jew," in "roaming through the earth in course of time reaches America, and finally Prince Edward Island. He finds the Island simply virgin forest, inhabited by a few savages. While musing one day in a sheltered glade, he is visited by an Angel, who rebukes him for his pessimistic outlook upon the future of the Island, and promises to return at the end of each hundred years, to compare with him the results of the preaching of the Gospel of Calvary, in its effect upon the development of the Island."[49] In 1927 Sidey's *Supplanter*, based on the life of Jacob, was performed at Bedeque and in the following year *The Pilgrim or the Torch of Truth*.[50] This latter pageant tried to describe the history of the Maritimes Home Missions from its beginnings in 1814. In the "Final Tableau," all the cast joined "in ascribing praise to the King of Kings, the World's Redeemer," while the congregation joined "in the singing of 'Crown Him with Many Crowns.'"[51] Sidey evidently hoped that this production would travel the United Baptist Convention circuit and thrust him a little closer to the centre of convention power and influence.[52]

Though widely performed, Sidey's productions did not bring him much power and influence on the mainland. He therefore decided to move closer to the Baptist heartland of Nova Scotia. In July 1930 he followed his dear friend J.B. Daggett to Kingston, Nova Scotia. Daggett's ill health had forced him to resign as pastor of the Kingston-Melvern Square-Lower Aylesford United Baptist churches. He persuaded his church to issue a call to Sidey who was eager to leave the Island, having – as Daggett delicately expressed it – "been unfortunate in his investments."[53] Certain persistent Island creditors were pressuring Sidey hard, and he was keen to escape the embarrassment and ill will produced by his unsuccessful business ventures in silver fox farming, especially as the dark gloom of the Great

Depression engulfed the Island. Moreover, he and his wife Edna had become a little bored with their Island ministry.

Less than a month after being inducted as pastor of the Kingston-Melvern Square-Lower Aylesford United Baptist churches, in the summer of 1930, Sidey organized the second annual Baptist Evangelical Bible Conference, which was held in his Kingston church. The stated purpose of the conference was "an outpouring of the Holy Ghost for power in soul winning upon the churches of the United Baptist Convention in the Maritime Provinces and upon every individual attending the Conference."[54] Among the Baptist ministers attending the conference were R.W. Lindsay, Upper Canard; Allan Tedford, of Woodstock; William B. Bezanson, Glace Bay; Henry T. Wright, Truro; and Horace L. Kinsman of Port Lorne. None of these ministers, it is important to note, had graduated from Acadia University and only Bezanson had a BD degree.[55] At the 1931 conference, the third one held at Kingston, Sidey, as principal organizer, was responsible for shifting the emphasis away from the "Baptism of the Holy Spirit" toward premillennialism. As Sidey put it in his official "Greetings" to the delegates, he was "daily looking forward to that Blessed Hope, the Rapture of the Church."[56] As had been the case in 1930 the Reverend Edward Morris, the Anglican evangelical from Halifax, was the key-note speaker, and only Reverend Wright from Truro, among the convention Baptist ministers who had attended the 1930 conference, was not there in 1931. Wright had left the region. The four other ministers, Lindsay, Tedford, Bezanson, and Kinsman, were joined by the Reverends F.C. Haysmere of Clementsvale, Alexander G. Crowe of Bedeque, J.H. Copeland of Nictaux, and T.A. Meister of Westchester. Most of these men would join Sidey and Daggett soon after they had left the convention in 1934.

Because of the "smouldering concern" of the conference delegates "for their denomination's veracity in the handling of the Scriptures" and their conviction that Acadia University, like McMaster University in Ontario, was a liberal-modernist stronghold, it was decided to establish the Kingston Bible College.[57] The college was like scores of other fundamentalist schools built throughout North America during the interwar years in order to protect what was regarded as the true "Biblical faith."[58] Sidey was named the first president of Kingston Bible College and he was to be assisted by Kinsman, Haysmere, and Daggett. The college was defined as an interdenominational, rather than as a Baptist institution, probably in order to appeal to a wider cross-section of potential students, but there were only three full-time students during the first year of the College's existence.

Thus by the autumn of 1931 Sidey, with Daggett's assistance, had created the framework for a parallel Baptist convention. They had their own publication, *The Gospel Light* established in 1931, to compete with the *Maritime Baptist*. They had the Kingston Bible College to train their men and women for their special evangelistic work in the region. Sidey and Daggett had their annual Baptist Evangelistic and Bible Conference, although Sidey was supported by fewer than a half-dozen Baptist congregations while the other convention could count on well over five hundred. Nonetheless, by 1932, all that Sidey needed was a little push to persuade him to leave the Maritime Baptist Convention. The push may have been provided by T.T. Shields and his former supporters in Ontario, who made it very clear that their continued financial support to Sidey was dependent on his quitting the convention. Furthermore, Sidey's Maritime followers were pushing him toward secession. They had had enough of what they regarded as the modernist convention and they were disgusted with what they heard was going on at Acadia.[59] According to them, divinity students were being taught that the Bible was not inerrant; it was like any other book. Their professors openly scoffed at the "divinity of the Lord," and at the Genesis view of Creation. Evolution was taught as the inspired gospel of the new scientific élite. And, to make matters even worse, dancing took place "regularly within Acadia's walls."[60] According to Daggett, his and Sidey's complaints about Acadia had fallen upon deaf ears. "We are looked upon as cranks and fanatics"[61] he observed, rather than as committed disciples of the Lord. Underscoring further the modernistic and even "Unitarian influences"[62] that controlled the convention and Acadia, Professor Shirley Case, a graduate of Acadia in 1893, the scourge of fundamentalism in the United States, Professor of Divinity at the University of Chicago, and eloquent advocate of theological liberalism, had been awarded the honourary DCL by Acadia University in 1928. According to Daggett, who knew Case personally, the native of New Brunswick, was "on the staff of the greatest infidel factory in America."[63] By awarding Case the honourary DCL degree, Acadia and the convention "had stamped approval upon the most rampant Modernistic Institution on the Continent of America."[64]

By the summer of 1933, it was obvious that the convention leaders had had enough of Sidey, Daggett, Kingston Bible College, and the intensifying attacks on their so-called "unadulterated Modernism."[65] The 1933 convention had decided to investigate certain charges concerning the general conduct of Sidey. On the surface what concerned the convention was that Sidey had refused to send it a certain sum of money raised for a specific convention purpose in his churches. Sidey, the evidence suggests, was guilty either of financial dishonesty or duplicity. But neither this fact nor his Oriental University DD was sufficient cause for his expulsion. His parallel convention was, as were his and Daggett's vitriolic attacks on the convention and Acadia.

On 10 or 11 November 1933, Sidey had decided to jump ship before being thrown off and so he wrote "a letter of resignation" to the convention.[66] By the middle of March 1934 his resignation was accepted by the Kingston and Lower Aylesford United Baptist churches but not by Melvern Square. A majority of members of the latter church, and significant minorities from the two former, left their churches along with Sidey to form the Independent Baptist Church. At their 1934 convention, the United Maritime Baptists accused Sidey of using "a bogus DD degree," and permitting "checks issued by him to be dishonoured by the bank on which they were drawn" and misapplying "denominational funds collected on the circuit at Kingston." In the judgment of the Examining Council, Sidey was felt "no longer worthy to have his name retained on the list of ordained ministers."[67] The convention also authorized its Executive Committee "to conserve the United Baptist interests at Malvern Square, Lewis Head [Shelburne County] and whenever necessary throughout the Convention"[68] Daggett's name was striken from the "list of ministers for cause" as was that of the Reverend F.S. Haysmere, the Baptist minister at Lewis Head, who was one of Sidey's Nova Scotia lieutenants.[69] What the convention did in 1934 was to accept formally the fact that Sidey, Daggett, Haysmere, and many of their followers had already quit. Thus secession became expulsion, and the Maritime United Baptist Convention indicated that it was prepared to fight the Sidey group in order to keep the schism in check.

Although the Kingston Bible College was forced to leave the Kingston United Baptist Church building, Sidey stubbornly held on to the parsonage. After a bitter court case in May 1935, the convention forced him out of the parsonage. The Kingston Baptist Parsonage Case, conducted in the Nova Scotia Supreme Court, Kentville, from 21 May to 25 May 1935, captured the attention of the entire province. It was not really a case about the ownership of a parsonage; rather it was a remarkable confrontation between two groups of Baptists, two ideologies, and two ways of life. It was essentially a battle between fundamentalism and a more accommodating spirit – what has been referred to as "a new hermaneutic" based on "a double commitment: to the Biblical faith on the one hand and to the modern outlook on the other."[70] This is not to suggest that the entire United Baptist Convention of the Maritime provinces was modernist; it obviously was not. Yet some of its leadership was certainly affected by the "Modernist impulse"[71] and so were a surprising number of its members. And throughout the 1930s the convention's major mouthpiece, *The Maritime Baptist*, was far more liberal than it was conservative, far more sympathetic to modernism than to fundamentalism.[72] There appeared to be a serious problem in the convention; Sidey had been determined to do something about it – even if it meant destroying the Maritime United Baptist Convention.

The Kingston Baptist Parsonage Case was heard by Mr Justice Humphry Mellish in the Supreme Court of Nova Scotia during the May 1935 term in Kentville. Over a four-day period, from 21-23 May and on 25 May, "No less than 50,000 words of evidence including testimony from as far back as 300 B.C." were heard.[73] For the *Halifax Herald* reporter, the packed courtroom "crowded with members of the clergy, church officials, and prominent laymen, resembled more the place of an important church meeting than a Supreme Court trial."[74] Not to be outdone, the *Halifax Chronicle* special correspondent maintained that the "intense interest" generated by the trial was "reminiscent of" that "at a murder trial."[75]

From the beginning, Sidey realized that, as he put it, the "real issue fought out in the Supreme Court of Nova Scotia was the issue between Modernism and Fundamentalism."[76] The question of the ownership of the Kingston parsonage was only the excuse for Sidey and his supporters to confront all convention Baptists with the awful truth that "the Convention" was "no longer Baptist but Unitarian, and in some cases, infidel."[77] And as far as Sidey was concerned he, like fundamentalist leaders such as J. Gresham Machen and T.T. Shields, was determined never to "bow the knee to the Baal of Modernism."[78] Scores of Sidey supporters had pushed themselves into the courtroom proudly carrying their Schofield Bibles – the badge of their fundamentalism – and their conviction that they were indeed supporting the Lord's anointed against the despised convention anti-Christ. The trial was their trial as well, and they desperately wanted the world to know where they stood. Also in the courtroom were convention officials and supporters who seemed not as intense and not as alienated as their opponents.

When Mr Justice Humphry Mellish entered the crowded courtroom he was met by what the *Halifax Chronicle* called "Batteries of leading legal talent."[79] Representing the convention plaintiffs were B.W. Roscoe KC, of Kentville, and George C. Nowlan, the former Tory MLA and former convention Baptist Young People's Union (BYPU) president. Opposing them and representing the trustees of the Kingston and Melvern Square Independent Baptist churches were T.R. Robertson KC of Halifax and J.E. Rutledge KC, both of Halifax, and R.E. Boylan of Berwick. Roscoe and Nowlan argued that the trustees of the Kingston and Melvern Square United Baptist churches, which had originally and jointly built the parsonage, still owned the building thought to be worth, in 1935, $3,800. Robertson, Rutledge, and Boylan, on the other hand, contended that the Independent Baptists were the true Baptists – the ones who still preached and practised what they called "Baptistic principles," and they therefore had the right to the parsonage. Their clients, however, had to admit that they had seceded from the United Baptist Church to create the Independent Baptist Church. This admission, in the final analysis, would completely destroy their case.

With the parsonage detail out of the way, Sidey and Daggett were ready to use this courtroom setting to strike hard at the convention – their principal objective. They naively thought that if they could prove to their own satisfaction that the convention, and especially Acadia University, were not orthodox, that thousands of Maritime Baptists would rally to the fundamentalist cause. There was a peculiar sense of hubris and self-importance permeating the testimonies of Sidey and Daggett. They were absolutely convinced of the rightness and righteousness of their cause; moreover, they felt that they were special instruments of the Almighty divinely chosen to return Maritime Protestantism to true Christianity. Feeling a tremendous sense of alienation from society because of the way in which the forces of modernity were altering their world, and experiencing both an acute collective paranoia and garrison mentality, they saw in the pure church ideal the means to deal with what they perceived to be the grim realities of twentieth-century life. J.B. Daggett declared in 1935 that "We are rushing with lightning speed toward the crisis, vividly foretold in the Book of Books. It behooves the Church of God to separate herself completely from the world, and the things of the world, and to be busy without holidays."[80] For Sidey, if Maritime Baptists did not abandon the "New Paganism" for "Fundamentalist separation and purity," they would be "the human cycle for the religion of Anti-Christ."[81]

Sidey was first questioned, on Wednesday 22 May, by his lawyer T.R. Robertson about his education, his preaching call, and what had transpired in the Kingston and Melvern Square United Baptist churches in the 1931 period.[82] Sidey made the point that his Independent Baptist Church alone espoused "the historic Baptist position" concerning church polity and explicity argued that, by leaving the convention, his church had become the true Baptist church and the convention had, by betraying Baptist independence, become non-Baptist. Sidey's cross-examination by George Nowlan did not go as smoothly as had his questioning by T.R. Robertson. Nowlan was a peculiar mixture of sophistication and almost bucolic opaqueness. Sometimes he could cut quickly and deftly to the heart of an issue and at other times he circled further and further away from the point being considered until the thrust of his questioning appeared to be totally irrelevant. Nowlan was very familiar with the United Baptist Convention, a familiarity which should have provided some edge to his Kentville performance.

Nowlan obviously disliked Sidey and Daggett, as his questioning and his comments made outside the courtroom show.[83] He wanted to paint Sidey in a bad light, and his questioning had little to do with the actual merits of the case involving the Kingston parsonage. Nowlan asked Sidey about Oriental University – "What was that?" "It purported to be a correspondence school, a university," Sidey replied. "You got in touch with them for what purpose?" "To see if I could do further work. I wanted to continue my work. I did seven or eight months work there. I got my M.A. degree for the thesis I submitted; I received my D.D." The courtroom was deathly quiet as Nowlan pressed the alumnus from Oriental University even further. "It was under charter? Why was it restrained?" he asked. "It was under charter and certain work was being done but I understood the restraining order was issued because it was not living up to its printed obligations" was the embarrassed reply. "It was fraudulent and the court stopped it!" Nowlan snapped at Sidey. "Did you ever see the institution?" "No, it was a correspondence course," Sidey answered.

Nowlan also questioned Sidey about his obtaining his "ordination certificate" from the United Baptist Convention after enduring a fifteen-minute period of questioning by an Examining Council chaired by Professor Dr Simeon Spidle, dean of theology at Acadia University. Sidey now contended that his 1927 decision to go before the convention's Examining Council was, in fact, "unBaptistic." He also stressed that the convention had abandoned the key Baptist belief that the Scriptures, in their original form, were divinely inspired and inerrant.

Q. Where are the original writings?
A. In the various copies of the New Testament.
Q. Where are the original writings?
A. Some in the British Museum and other libraries throughout the world.
Q. The original writings?
A. The earliest copies we have.
Q. I am asking where the original writings are.
A. I don't know.
Q. Do you know of any record of them ever being found?
A. I don't know. There are translations.
Q. From what date?
A. 325, 350 A.D.
Q. That would be some three hundred years after some of the events they detailed?
A. Certainly.
Q. And these manuscripts are in what?
A. Greek and other oriental writings.
Q. They in turn have been translated into ours?
A. Yes.
Q. How old are the oldest documents in the Old Testament?
A. 200 years B.C., I could not say; 300 B.C. translated into Hebrew; I think the Latin is the oldest and that is 380 B.C.
Q. And that records historical events that happened long ago?
A. It contains writings inspired by God.

Q. You say it is necessary to accept that?

A. I say the Holy Spirit of God gave these writings to the world, inspired men to write them, and the same Holy Spirit that gave it has guarded and kept that word so we can follow it as God intended.

Q. You say it is necessary to accept this?

A. Absolutely.

Q. You make that an absolute precedent to entering the church?

A. That is the condition of membership. I say that would be a condition of membership in any church of which I was pastor.

In this toe-to-toe confrontation, Sidey probably got the better of Nowlan, since Sidey was unable to present a moderate fundamentalist position, and Nowlan did not ask the most important question: What is the so-called traditional Baptistic position *vis-à-vis* the inspiration of the scriptures and church membership?

Nowlan then turned to the Bible College – what the *Halifax Herald* referred to as "a vital factor in the action"[84] – and forced Sidey to admit that there might have been a connection between his leaving the convention and the promise of financial assistance for the college from anti-convention Baptists in Toronto. This was an important admission and one that must have delighted convention officials. Nowlan then immediately pressed his advantage by asking Sidey "You did make the suggestion that you would like to teach evangelism at Acadia at one time? "I deny it," answered Sidey, "I was talking to Dr. Spidle about the advisability of an evangelistic Bible school. As for my going on the faculty of Acadia I was not expecting it; my work is in the field. If it was mentioned the wrong construction was put on it. I remember talking it over purely from that standpoint; I had no thought of what you suggest. I did suggest a good Bible school in connection with the Convention would be a good thing." There was enough in Sidey's response to suggest that he was something of a sore loser. The same thing had been said about T.T. Shields. If he had been offered a McMaster position in 1922 or 1923, it was widely asserted in convention circles, he still would have been in the convention in 1935.

Nowlan ended his examination of Sidey with a series of questions concerning the latter's fundamental beliefs, and then B.W. Roscoe took over from a flagging Nowlan. He asked Sidey how he had dealt with the "allotment of contributions to the funds of the Convention."

Sidey had to confess that his three churches had, in fact, raised $290.75 for convention purposes but that he had sent only $150 to the convention. Roscoe then asked Sidey "Will you tell the court if that is not one of the reasons for your retiring from the United Baptist Convention?" "No, sir," was the answer – nothing more nothing less. But another seed of doubt had been planted in Kentville.

Daggett was put on the witness stand on Thursday, 23 May, by J.E. Rutledge, one of his lawyers. Daggett, the former Free Baptist minister, was confident, aggressive, and impressive in his performance – far more so than Sidey had been. According to Daggett, even before leaving the convention he had often declared that "the students at Acadia were filled up with unBaptistic teaching, especially the hypothesis of evolution." Moreover, Acadia "conferred honourary degrees" on the most "unBaptistic" of men. Daggett again emphasized the importance of the independence of the local church and the evils of any form of interdependence. In addition, he condemned dancing and card playing. As far as his "scriptural authority" for such a stance and for his anti-Acadia feelings, Daggett declared, as he thumbed quickly through his Bible:

I would like to close with a word of scripture in this connection. We will turn to First John, second chapter and 22nd verse "Who is a liar but he that denieth that Jesus is the Christ? He is anti-Christ that denieth the Father and the Son"; then First John 4th Chapter, beginning at the second verse "Hereby know ye the Spirit of God: Every spirit that confesseth that Jesus Christ is come in the flesh is of God"; and turn to Second John 7th verse, "For many deceivers are come into the world who confess not that Jesus Christ is come in the flesh. This is a deceiver and an anti-Christ." Our Convention has received men and honoured them who deny in the most blasphemous manner that Jesus Christ is the son of God. Then I dare not stay in the Convention lest I become a partaker in their evil ways.

In his cross-examination Nowlan wondered why Daggett's earlier Free-Baptist view of the importance of the ordination councils had changed, and Daggett had to admit that since the creation of the United Maritime Baptist Convention this had been convention policy and that he had played a key role in pushing the convention in this direction. Nowlan then asked Daggett to explain "the Fundamentals." As far as Sidey's lieutenant was concerned "verbal inspiration" of the Bible was the key fundamentalist tenet. "What are the other fundamentals?" he was asked. "Belief in the scriptures as verbally inspired." He stressed

that all scripture was given by the Holy Spirit and is not open to any private interpretation; that it is the word of the living God; we believe that Jesus Christ was God revealed in the flesh; that he was God's special gift as a mediator between himself and man, and upon the cross He bore our sins and that his blood cleanses us of all sins if we confess our sins, cleanses us of unrighteousness; next that he rose from the dead physically that he ascended on high physically; that he is to-day our advocate at the right hand of the Father. We believe his physical body's not moved by blood but by the spirit.

An exasperated Nowlan interrupted Daggett with the comment "I am just asking for fundamentals." Daggett effortlessly described his premillennialist view, that before Christ "returns to the world to rule the nations of the earth his voice will be heard and the dead in Christ shall rise first." "I am asking for your fundamental beliefs," Nowland pressed "which you accept; I want to know what they are." It was as though Daggett was oblivious to Nowlan's interjection. "Next," he went on, "his physical return, when he shall come to rule the nations of the earth for a thousand years, that is the premillennial view." "That is a fundamental?" "No man can be a Christian who does not accept God manifest in the flesh in Jesus Christ, and a man to be a real member of the church must be born again of the Holy Ghost. That is what we believe." For Daggett "these were" his "fundamental beliefs."

B.W. Roscoe's cross-examination stressed Daggett's involvement in the 1917 New Brunswick Patriotic Potato Scandal. Roscoe asked Daggett a barbed question. "You were very vehement in your remarks against evil doings and partakers in evil. Have you always been as careful in that regard?" He went on, "You were not so careful when you were Deputy Minister of Agriculture in New Brunswick." "I was," Daggett bravely replied. Then Roscoe threw at Daggett the charge that had been reverberating throughout Nova Scotia and New Brunswick for months. "Is it right to deposit monies in a name other than your own to the extent of thirty-five thousand dollars? That is what you did when you were Deputy Minister of Agriculture in New Brunswick." "Under what name?" Daggett asked. "William

Thompson, was it not?" came the reply, to which Daggett could only respond "Yes, I did, and it was perfectly legitimate too." The feisty, combative preacher was unrepentant and on the offensive when others would have collapsed in despair. When given an opportunity later in the day to clarify his involvement in the scandal, Daggett emphasized that he had been duped by the "chief manipulator of the Conservative party." To protect himself from any possible charges of theft, Daggett had deposited $35,000 in a bank under an assumed name and, as far as he was concerned, the McQueen Commission Report had completely exonerated him. And, in concluding his testimony, Daggett thundered that "no one but a slanderer and a rascal would bring it up."

On Saturday, 25 May, the convention decided to put forward its case against the Sidey-Daggett fundamentalist critique. Two men were selected for this important task, Dr G.C. Warren, editor of the *Maritime Baptist*, and Dr Simeon Spidle, perhaps the most powerful and influential person in the convention. Warren testified first.[85] Born in 1884 on Prince Edward Island, Warren was educated at Prince of Wales College, Charlottetown, at Acadia University, and Newton Theological Seminary, Massachusetts, from which seminary he received his BD degree in 1912. He pastored Baptist churches in Bridgetown and at Brunswick Street, Fredericton. In 1929 he was appointed editor of the *Maritime Baptist*. In 1936 he became a member of the Faculty of Theology at Acadia and in 1942 its dean. As editor of the *Maritime Baptist*, Warren was far more sympathetic to the so-called modernist side than to the fundamentalist. He regularly reprinted articles written by very liberal theologians from England and the United States – men like Nathaniel Micklem, L.H. Marshall, and Shirley Case[86] – but never printed any material authored by any key North American fundamentalist. Under questioning from Nowlan, Robertson, and Rutledge, Warren contended that Baptist congregational independence was always balanced by associational interdependence and he stressed the crucial role played by the convention in the ordination process. In his concluding testimony Warren maintained that "as soon as the Baptists developed they said: We are not isolated entities, there is fellowship, and they formed the Association [in Nova Scotia] in 1800."

Simeon Spidle followed Warren to the witness stand.[87] Spidle was born in New Cornwall in 1867. After graduating from Acadia with a BA degree in 1897, he served two Baptist pastorates, in Cape Breton and at Falmouth. He received his BD from Newton Theological Seminary in 1903 and his PHD in Philosophy from Clark University in Worcester, Massachusetts, in 1911. In 1911 he was also appointed professor of philosophy, systematic theology and church history at Acadia and then in 1922 its Dean of Theology, a position he held until 1936 when he retired. Spidle was the general factotam in the convention during the 1920s and early 1930s. He was a key member of the Examining Council and almost singlehandedly determined who would and who could not be ordained as ministers in the convention. An ardent believer in the importance of an educated ministerial élite, he attempted, often without much success, to impose his high academic standards on the convention. Spidle was neither a fundamentalist nor a liberal but rather what might be termed a liberal evangelical. He accepted much of the critical Biblical scholarship but without abandoning his belief in the divinity of Christ, regeneration, miracles, and immortality. As a scholar, he refused to see things solely in black and white terms but rather frequently saw huge grey patches. He did not perform particularly well in Kentville on 25 May 1935, perhaps because of his tendency to avoid answering certain questions directly and honestly. George Nowlan asked Spidle to comment on Sidey's contention that "verbal inspiration of the scriptures" was "a pre-requisite to membership in the Baptist church in the Maritime Provinces." "To make it a pre-requisite" or a belief in any form of millennialism," Spidle answered, "is entirely an unbaptistic procedure."

Rutledge's cross-examination was a little more contentious than Nowlan's probing had been. He zeroed in on Spidle's theology. What did Spidle mean when he stated that the "Old and New Testament Scriptures were written by men divinely inspired – by whom?" "By the spirit of God," Spidle responded. "Is that not, in all fairness, the doctrine of verbal inspiration?" he was asked. "No, not by any means," Spidle replied. "I say verbal inspiration means this, that the very words and ideas were dictated to the minds of the writers; that the writers themselves had nothing to do with creating the ideas or the language." Rutledge then asked Spidle whether he believed there was an actual "dictation to Moses." "Cite the case" Spidle retorted. "What I have reference particularly to is the making of the ten commandments." "There's nothing said there about dictation," was the curt reply.

After reiterating that a premillennial belief had never been a "pre-requisite to membership" in any Maritime Baptist Convention church, Spidle was urged by Rutledge to clarify his view of inspiration. "Do you accept the scriptures from Genesis to Revelation as being verbally inspired and of God yourself?" "No, certainly not," Spidle answered. "What do you say?" "I hold to the historic theory of the inspiration of the Bible," Spidle replied. "How do you define that?" Acadia's Dean of Theology quickly retorted: "Co-operation of the spirit of God and the mind of man arriving at the religious truth incorporated in the Bible." Before Spidle could get himself any deeper in difficulty Nowlan jumped to his feet and argued that "the individual views of the witness are immaterial." He was sustained, and Rutledge shifted to a few seemingly irrelevant questions about Acadia before returning to theological issues by asking, "Do you preach and teach the virgin birth of Christ?" Once again, Nowlan objected to the line of questioning, and Rutledge agreed not to "press the question." But he did press Spidle on the question of whether he believed "that Christ was divine." "I certainly do," answered the Acadia's Dean of Theology.

Q. Do you believe and teach he was the Deity?

A. He was divine in the sense that there was in him the divine quality of life.

Q. The efficacy of the Blood Atonement – what is generally meant by that?

A. It is spoken of in the usual way as the substitution of Christ for the sinner; I don't know if that is what they mean by blood atonement.

Q. Do you believe that the death of Christ upon the cross was by way of atonement of sins?

A. I surely do, but you must remember there are no fewer than twelve different theories. The substitution is one of them, which is that the sufferings of Christ were a punishment inflicted on Christ the innocent in place of the guilty; that the innocent was punished for the guilty and the guilty were allowed to go free.

Q. The bodily resurrection of our Lord: Do you teach and preach a physical resurrection?

A. I think there is no doubt about the New Testament preaching that; I have no quarrel with the teachings of the New Testament.

Q. Do you believe in the physical return of Jesus?

A.   That is a doctrine that is held by Baptists, that there will be a return
of Christ to this earth.

It was clear to everyone in the courtroom that Spidle had tried to
avoid the question. So Rutledge asked again "Do you preach and
teach a physical return?" "I never use that in any of my preaching
because I don't think it is an important matter to emphasize in
teaching; our business is to carry on the work and when the time
arrives he will come." Spidle was asked on a number of occasions
to define modernism and fundamentalism but he stubbornly refused
to do so. Rutledge then asked him if he knew the University of
Chicago theologian Dr Shirely Case. Spidle did. He was then asked
if he considered Case a "modernist or a fundamentalist?" "I am not
labelling any man," he shot back. Spidle was asked why Case had
been given an honourary DCL by Acadia in 1928. It was, suggested
Spidle, because of Case's close association with Horton Academy
where he had once taught. Spidle was then requested to listen to a
statement to be found on page eighty of Case's *Jesus Through the
Centuries*.

The spark that ignited the tinder of a new faith for Peter was the need felt
within himself during the crucifixion, for his former leader's reinstatement
in divine favor. The notion of Jesus' apotheosis, so readily suggested by
popular Gentile religions in Peter's environment, brought to him too valuable a relief from his perplexity and too vivid an assurance of future help
to leave any room for questioning the propriety of his procedure. Peter did
not actually believe that a deceased man had become a god. No Jew however, unschooled, could have assented to any such affirmation. It remained
for his Greek successors in the new religion to recognize in Jesus a full
fledged christian deity ... Strictly speaking, this risen Jesus was not an
absolute deity; he was only a messianized hero.

"Would you say that was in any way fundamentalistic?" Rutledge
asked. "I will let the fundamentalist say whether it is or not," was
the curt reply. Similar responses were given to questions about three
other quotations from Case's writings.

Rutledge wondered how any orthodox Baptist university could
confer an honourary degree on a person like Case, whose modernist
views were so well known. In reply Spidle stressed that "The degree
was not conferred upon him for his theological views but because

he was a teacher in the academy whose centenary was being cele-
brated." Again, Rutledge endeavoured to pressure Spidle into admitting that Case was a modernist. There was, understandably, a
biting edge to the lawyer's question "Do you mean seriously to say,
as an educationist of this province, you do not care to answer a
simple question in regard to extracts I have read as being the work
of a fundamentalist or modernist?" "I make no pronouncements on
the matter," was Spidle's response. The final question from Rutledge
was "Does Acadia, as a university, teach organic evolution?" "That
belongs to the Department of Biology. I am not a member of that
Department," answered Spidle. This was not Dean Spidle's finest
hour. Perhaps his defensiveness is understandable; but his stubborn
refusal to admit the obvious – that Case was a modernist – is almost
incomprehensible.

The final arguments were presented to Mr Justice Mellish in
Halifax on 26 June 1935. Robertson and Rutledge argued that the
Melvern Square Independent Baptist Church should receive $1450
from the sale of the parsonage, and $2350 should go to the Kingston
United Baptists. Nowlan and Roscoe, on the other hand, contended
that the entire sum should go to the two United Baptist congregations. The Independents had seceded and had no right to the property which still belonged to the convention churches. On 16
September Mr Justice Mellish declared in favour of the convention
Baptists. As far as costs were concerned, which according to Judge
Mellish, "have been considerable when considered in relation to the
value of the property involved," judgment was reserved.[88] In late
1935 Mellish awarded the convention Baptists $548 for "court ex-
penses," rubbing more salt in the wounds of the Independents.[89]

Even while Judge Mellish was preparing his judgment, in the
summer of 1935, Sidey was receiving reports from missionaries he
had sent out to all corners of the Maritimes and to Newfoundland
under the auspices of the International Christian Mission, which he
had established in March 1935. He named himself chief commis-
sioner and editor of the ICM's monthly publication, *The Question*.
Daggett continued to edit the *Gospel Light*. Sidey announced in the
March 1935 issue of *The Question* that "denominationalism as such
through its organizations and ecclesiastical control has had its day
and like many other institutions hoary with age, it is now practically
a wreck on the shores of time, devoid both of spiritual power and
truth ... The Mission is not a church but rather a soul saving, Bible

teaching, witnessing organization." The college was to train Sidey's missionaries who then would establish congregations of true Christian believers in all parts of the Maritimes and also in "foreign lands." Expecting an imminent rapture of the saints, Sidey and Daggett were determined to do all in their power to telescope the last days into a brief apocalyptic moment.

Two young men, William Freeman and Hilbourne Redden, were sent to the Canso area; two others, Eric Monevan and Henry Crocker, to Hants County; four women, Mildred Neily, Ethel Skarling, Ethel Thompson, and Kizbro Dulliver to the Yarmouth region, and Margaret Tedford to Carleton County; Julian Green was located in Kings County, Nova Scotia; Nancy Nelson and Winona Beylea, in Moncton; and William Norton in Kentville. These young men and women associated themselves with independent Baptist ministers, such as Maxwell Bolser and Orden Stairs in Shelburne County, Russel Lynds and T.A. Meister in Colchester County, Clifford Barkhouse in Cumberland County, Sadie Reid on Prince Edward Island, and Allen Tedford in Truro. All of these young men and women had close connections with Sidey and his Baptist supporters, especially those in Nova Scotia.

Excluding his Kingston team, Sidey had no fewer than twenty ardent disciples working for his cause in the three Maritime provinces in the summer of 1935. Financial support for the work came not only from the region but also from Central Canada and the United States. Velma Crummie was also preaching the Sidey-Daggett gospel in Conception Bay, Newfoundland. Faced with all these independent Baptist ministers and ICM missionaries at work in the region, convention Baptists became increasingly concerned, and the convention leaders began a well-planned counter-offensive at the grass-roots level, against what they spitefully referred to as "tramp preachers."[90] At the Eastern United Baptist Association meetings held in Sydney in July 1935, these outsiders were condemned for "endeavouring to poison the minds of our people and destroy their faith." All convention ministers were therefore urged "to inaugurate a campaign in our churches, which will educate to a greater degree than exists today the rank and file of our members and adherents as regards the origin, principles and polity of Baptist people.[91] At the August 1935 United Baptist Convention, the Home Missions Committee reported that "Disturbing agencies are busy in an effort to undo the work of the Christian Church." "Men who have no connection with our body" it was observed, "are brazenly appearing in our churches and whether locally received or rejected carry on a campaign well calculated to destroy the church life." "In some cases," and this was particularly true in the Canso area, and in Shelburne County, "such a campaign assumes the nature of a house to house canvass in an attempt to have our Baptist people withdraw from our Baptist work and fellowship."[92]

The convention counter-attack was particularly successful in New Brunswick and the Yarmouth region. Sometimes with the assistance of the local police, convention leaders expelled certain Sideyites from convention churches, pushing back the Sidey forces to key bridge-heads in the Canso area and in Shelburne County. These were the areas where the Sideyites had their greatest strength, outside the Kingston region, in the late 1930s and 1940s. The Reverend Tedford was to be forced out of the Emmanuel Baptist Church, Truro, to be replaced by the dynamic and conservative evangelical supporter of the convention, Abner Langley. The Reverend Neil Herman and his nephew, the Reverend Arthur Herman, were the two other outspoken Sidey supporters in the convention. In 1936 Neil was eased out of West End, Halifax, and in that same year became the field secretary for the anti-Acadian "English-speaking League of New Brunswick." Three years later he emigrated to Florida. His nephew, who was the minister at Highfield Street, Moncton, remained in his church until 1938, sullen, critical, yet unwilling to leave the convention.[93]

The Sidey schism did not, however, result in a significant haemorrhage of members from convention churches. In 1934 the New Brunswick resident membership was 21,090, non-resident membership 7,357; the Nova Scotia membership, including the Black churches, was 20,856 residents and 7,953 non-residents; and Prince Edward Island 1,542 residents and 479 non-residents. By 1936, the New Brunswick resident membership had risen to 21,103 and non-resident to 8,025, and in Nova Scotia the resident to 21,179, while the non-resident had dropped to 7,793. In Prince Edward Island, there was a slight increase in both categories, to 1,620 and 481. In 1936, there were 1,736 baptisms reported while in 1934 there had only been 1,368 and, in 1935, only 1,377. In 1936, some 672 members had been dismissed by letter, compared to 590 in 1935 and 546 in 1934, but most of the increase was not due to the Sideyite secession movement. In 1933 before the Sidey-convention confrontation, no fewer than 736 members had been "dismissed by letter" and, in 1941, a few years after, 635. The Depression and its immediate results, emigration, as well as World War II, would have a far more significant immediate and long-term impact on the convention than did J.J. Sidey.[94]

Why was the Maritime Baptist Convention able to deal so effectively with the Sidey secessionist threat? Why was the Sidey-convention confrontation not a crucial turning point in the history of the Maritime Baptist Church? Why did not the confrontation first disorient and then immobilize the convention, as had been the case with the Baptists in other regions of Canada and in the Northern United States? Even though there probably had been a "cosmopolitan/local" polarization in the convention in the late 1920s and early 1930, this polarization did not lead to a major split as it had in Ontario, British Columbia, and the Northern United States.[95] When a split did occur in a specific congregation, there is no evidence to suggest that class tension was at the core of the conflict. The most important factor was how specific people reacted to Sidey as a person.

The convention was a heterogenous mix of people and theologies. On the extremes of the theological spectrum were to be found fundamentalist and modernist groups and then, moving from the former to the latter, there were important groups of conservative evangelicals and liberal evangelicals. The conservative evangelicals felt as strongly as the fundamentalists about the so-called fundamentals of the faith but, on two key issues, they differed, and these two issues created the necessary theological space – what Freud called narcissism of small differences – between the two groups. Most United Baptist conservative evangelicals did not accept the central importance of premillennialism, nor did they feel particularly at home within the context of the powerful anti-cultural and anti-societal viewpoints of the fundamentalists. In other words, the conservative evangelicals were not as alienated from societal norms as were the fundamentalists, and they saw little psychological and spiritual need to retreat from Maritime and Canadian society to the safety of sectarian purity. Liberal evangelicals tried to balance evangelical spirituality and liberal learning; theirs was a religion of the heart and head. They refused to abandon the revivalist traditions of the Baptist patriarchs, but they also refused to close their eyes and their ears to modern scholarship. Of course, most Maritime

Baptists, whether members of the United Baptist Convention or merely adherents, did not spend much time or energy making fine theological distinctions. They were very much part of the Maritime Baptist mainstream – stretching back to the late eighteenth century – which had always placed far more emphasis on "promoting a good Work" than upon theological "Principles."[96] For these people continuity was far more appealing than abrupt change, as was a certain degree of liberal openness over an almost paranoid restrictiveness.[97] As a result Sidey found it extremely difficult to strike a responsive chord in the convention. Moreover, Sidey was an outsider to it. He was certainly not the kind of person one might have expected would try so valiantly to return twentieth-century Maritime Baptists to the purity of their early nineteenth-century Calvinist and evangelical past. He was not really familiar with the Maritime Baptist historical and religious legacy, and the nineteenth-century heroes of the Maritime Baptists – the patriarchs such as Edward and James Manning, Harris Harding, Theodore Seth Harding, Joseph Dimock, among others – were not part of his religious heritage. Consequently he was neither successful nor effective in his attempt to make his schismatic movement into a twentieth-century version of an Allinite-Manning Church. Nor was Sidey able to strike a responsive chord with fellow Maritimers at a time when they were experiencing the white-heat of the Maritime Rights Movement, for Sidey was not a Maritimer. He was British-born, educated in the United States, and in most respects an outsider. In addition, he was not even an ordained Baptist minister; he had been originally ordained as an American Methodist Episcopal minister and only became a Baptist minister after permanently settling in the Maritimes and after the creation of the United Church of Canada in 1925. His Methodist ordination had been simply accepted in 1925 by his new Prince Edward Island Baptist congregation, and Sidey had never felt the need to be re-ordained. In no significant way an integral part of the Maritime Baptist mainstream in the 1920s and 1930s, Sidey was not an especially brilliant organizer nor was he widely perceived as a charismatic leader. It is true that he was an enthusiastic and committed minister of the gospel; he was articulate, a very effective preacher, a persuasive polemicist, and ardently committed to the fundamentalist point of view. Finally, his wife, Edna, had caused her husband great difficulty and heartache. An independent woman of great ability, Edna Sidey was never intimidated by her husband

and, on at least one occasion, she had left him – and left him humiliated and angry. This kind of marital discord did little to help the fundamentalist cause in the Maritime provinces.

Another possible reason for Sidey's failure to become the Shields of the Maritimes was his inability to harness New Brunswick discontent over the convention and to direct it against the Nova Scotia convention leaders. Since the early nineteenth century, the ethos of the New Brunswick Baptists had been quite different from that of the Nova Scotia Baptists, and for decades they had resented the hegemony the Nova Scotians imposed upon the convention. Yet Sidey had no effective base in New Brunswick; his New Brunswick-born lieutenant, Daggett, was a source of weakness not strength, because of his involvement in the notorious 1917 scandal. Whenever Sidey tried to send his missionaries to New Brunswick they confronted strident opposition. The New Brunswick Baptist leaders had a greater fear and suspicion of Sidey than they did of the convention leaders in Nova Scotia, even those at Acadia University. They had great freedom within the convention and though they might criticize the liberalism of Acadia they saw no good reason to quit the convention in which they still exerted a great deal of influence. In New Brunswick, the Sidey forces not only confronted opposition in the convention – from fundamentalist, conservative and liberal evangelicals, and modernists – but also from other small sectarian Baptist groups, such as the Reformed Baptists, the Primitive Baptists, and some Free Baptists, groups with roots thrust deep into New Brunswick life and society. The Sideyites were no match for these New Brunswick sectarian Baptists. Nor could they compete with the growing Pentecostal movement.

A further reason for Sidey's relative lack of success was the vigorous counter-offensive mounted by convention leaders such as Spidle, Warren, and Dr E.S. Mason, superintendent of Home Missions. Initially, they had met the theological challenge posed by the Sidey group by persuading the convention to accept in 1934 "its unshaken loyalty to the historic principles of our Denomination including the Lordship of Christ, the inspiration of the Scriptures, the separation of church and state, the necessity of a regenerative life, and exemplary character and the autonomy and co-operate fellowship of the individual churches."[98] At the local level, especially at the association level, the convention leaders urged their followers to battle against Sidey's "tramp evangelists." One implicit argument presented to the convention ministers during the difficult Depression years proved particularly compelling. If the Sidey evangelists were successful, convention ministers would no longer have churches to minister to and, therefore, no salaries. Economic survival, as well as the threat to community prestige, helped bolster these ministers' determination to push back the sectarian invaders. And the Kingston Parsonage Case, which was won by the convention, seriously weakened the Sidey forces. Sidey reluctantly admitted this fact in the fall of 1935 when he witnessed a downturn in the number of students at the Kingston Bible College, as well as widespread concern, even among his most ardent followers, that the Independent Baptist Church had been relegated to the status of an "illegal church."[99] Making very effective use of local newspapers, Spidle and others viciously and personally attacked Sidey and Daggett describing them as dishonest, selfish, and unChristian leaders.[100] Some of these charges, however unfair, accomplished the desired end, as did the expulsion from the convention of unrepentant pro-Sidey ministers. Finally, in order to reassert its position at the evangelical core of the Baptist cause in the region, the convention in the post-1934 period placed a great deal of stress on evangelization. Over and over again, on the pages of the *Maritime Baptist*, local congregations were urged not only to pray for but to work diligently for a revival. Articles and editorials with titles such as "Need of Revival," "Revival Needed," and "Evangelism Needed" were printed and reprinted. Attempts were made to link the Maritime Baptists of the late 1930s with Henry Alline and the region's First Great Awakening.[101] This was something which Sidey never attempted to do; he had never even tried to use the Baptist historical heritage to infuse his movement with pride, respectability, and tradition. As an outsider he was never able to really understand the conservative ethos of the Maritime provinces.

A final reason for Sidey's failure to split the convention was the fact that Baptist mainstream theology in the Maritimes had always been basically syncretic, placing particular stress on personal religious experience and not on a specific religious ideology. It was the religion of Henry Alline and Harris Harding and not that of Gresham Machem or T.T. Shields. Most Maritime Baptists in the 1920s and 1930s could not really empathize with the main North American fundamentalist or modernist propagandists, because they perceived religion in a radically different manner. Unlike many of their Baptist cousins in Central Canada and the West, they had not, as yet, experienced the profound Americanization of their popular culture and were quite successful in the interwar years in resisting the fundamentalist-modernist bombardment from the south. Is it surprising that the two Baptist conventions in Canada most greatly influenced by the osmosis of Americanization were the two conventions most significantly affected by the fundamentalist-modernist controversy? In the final analysis, Sidey may not have been able to emulate Shields because he was too American for Maritime tastes. He had accommodated, too deeply, the habits of his mind to the Manichean theological world of Chicago in the immediate post-World-War-II period.

By late 1935, Sidey realized that his attempt to split the convention had failed. Yet he refused to be immobilized by the events of 1934 and 1935. He seemed even more enthusiastic about his Kingston area churches, more committed to his Bible college and the International Christian Mission. He became increasingly active in the Nova Scotia Sons of Temperance as well the Canadian Protestant League. Yet, despite his energy and sense of commitment, he was not even able to channel in his own organization the forces of sectarianism he had helped to unleash in the Kingston area. His college went through a number of painful schisms as faculty members left, outraged at Sidey's enthusiasm for Pentecostalism one year or his obsession with British Israelitism during another.[102] They felt that he was betraying his fundamentalist principles. Some of his independent Baptist followers stubbornly refused to toe his line and attacked his college and the ICM because they were not Baptist organizations. These people felt that Sidey had too readily sacrificed his Baptist principles on the altar of interdenominationalism. Although he had played a key role in organizing the Independent Baptist Churches in the Cape Sable area of Shelburne County, in Guysborough County, and in Westchester, Cumberland County, as well as in the Bedeque area of Prince Edward Island, by 1939 most of the Nova Scotia Independent Baptist churches had split away from Sidey. It was ironic that Sidey experienced a far worse secession from him in the late 1930s than had the United Baptist Convention.

When Sidey formed the Maritime Fellowship of Independent Baptists in 1940, in order to "provide a way whereby the Baptists (Ind) of the Maritime Provinces may find fellowship together,"[103] he was only able to attract to the organization his Kingston area Independent

Baptist Church and the tiny Coddle Harbour Baptist Church from Guysborough County. In 1962, his own Melvern Square Independent Church – including his wife Edna – split with the secessionist group to form a Fellowship Baptist Church. Four years later, Sidey, a spent-force, died. He had seen his Independent Baptist world collapse around him; his college was still in reasonable shape despite a tragic fire in 1962 but his ICM was little more than a postal address – a paper missionary society. Within two years of his death his tiny, fragile Maritime Fellowship of Independent Baptists was formally disbanded.

After his death on 23 May 1966, Sidey was described by Pastor Perry F. Rockwood, a former Presbyterian and a fundamentalist preacher in Nova Scotia, as "probably the pioneer separationist of the Maritimes."[104] One of his faithful deacons and a dear friend, E.E. Skaling, from Greenwood, praised Sidey as "a man of faith, a man who knew how to get answers to a prayer, a good friend and a Christian gentleman."[105] In the 1930s, it may be argued, J.J. Sidey represented the way the mainstream of the Maritime Baptists could have but did not follow. In the short run Sidey may have been the loser but in the long run, as the Maritime Baptist Convention and the Acadia Divinity College became increasingly conservative in their orientation and as the 1960s blurred into the 1970s, Sidey may well have come out the winner after all.

3 In Search of T.T. Shields' Impact on the Maritime Baptists in the 1920s and 1930s

Thomas Todhunter Shields was, without question, one of the two or three most influential Protestant leaders in Canada in the first half of the twentieth century. More than this, Shields was, as the key American liberal Protestant periodical the *Christian Century* of 29 May 1929 accurately put it, "unquestionably the dominant personality" among *all* North American fundamentalists. T.T. Shields was either loved or hated, respected or detested, considered as a true "disciple of Christ" or as a "minion of Antichrist." There appeared to be no middle-ground reaction to him among those who knew the extraordinarily gifted Baptist preacher and polemicist. One of his early disciples, Dr Morley Hall, captured Shield's polarizing tendency in a story he once told about two women in the Jarvis Street Baptist Church, Toronto, who were struck by the special effect of a shaft of morning sunshine on the countenance of the Reverend T.T. Shields as he sat piously behind his pulpit. "One was impressed by the angelic look on her pastor's face," Hall recounted. "The other was certain that she saw traces of the demonic."[1] In 1931 Jean Graham, a perceptive *Saturday Night* reporter, also captured the Janus-like quality of Shields:

Could this gentleman of benign countenance and mellifluous voice be the turbulent pastor who hated his enemies and loathed his theological opponents until he became wrathy and violent and longed for the Lord to destroy them? Surely there must be some mistake. As the sermon progressed the bewilderment increased. It was what would be called a simple gospel sermon, with no reference to modernists or other monstrosities ... During the week following he appeared to go on a rampage of malice and hatred and uncharitableness. Who is the true Dr. Shields? Is he the kindly Christian or the peevish propagandist?[2]

Six years before Shields died, in 1955, Gerald Anglin wrote a discerning article in *Maclean's* entitled "The Battling Baptist."[3] According to Anglin, Shields had changed very little during the almost two decades since the *Saturday Night* article. If anything, the bifurcation of Shields' personality had become more pronounced and his attacks on modernism more vitriolic and bizarre. From his pulpit in 1949, Shields

had gone scalping after gamblers, card players, burlesque comedians, the U.S. of A., and women. He has attacked beverage rooms ("trapdoors to hell"), bobbed hair ("The Lord never intended women to go to the barber") and athletics ("The Lord hath no pleasure in the legs of a man") ... he has denounced Methodists, Anglicans, the United Church, and the Oxford Group. More than any of these he has attacked the Roman Catholic Church – but he has lashed out at brother Baptists more relentlessly and more vehemently than at all other objects of his wrath combined.

Yet, it should be pointed out, the animus directed by Shields at his former Baptist friends was often balanced in his sermons with a heavy emphasis upon what might be called a Christocentric Calvinism.

There was certainly, as many have observed, a certain "Dr. Jekyll and Mr. Hyde" quality to T.T. Shields and his almost Manichean temperament.[4] Though widely regarded as one of the finest preachers in North America in the first half of the twentieth century,[5] Shields could also be a closed-minded bigot. His censorious sermons often lacked even a touch of Christian charity. Even though he always and proudly regarded the Bible as the infallible Word of God, he seldom permitted the Christ of the New Testament to excise what the great British preacher, Martyn Lloyd-Jones, once referred to as "this cancer ... of a wrong spirit and wrong methods" from his powerful message.[6]

Thomas Todhunter Shields was born in Bristol, England, in 1873, the fifth of eight children.[7] His father, originally a Methodist, was eventually ordained a Baptist minister and emigrated with his family in 1888 to pastor a small Baptist church in western Ontario. After his conversion in his father's church in 1891, T.T. Shields was ordained a Baptist minister "without the benefit of either a college or a seminary education."[8] After serving a number of Baptist churches in western Ontario, T.T. Shields was called to the prestigious Jarvis Street pastorate in Toronto. He remained as pastor of this church until his death in 1955.

C. Allyn Russell has described Shields' remarkable career in the following manner:

In addition to his long pastorate at Jarvis Street (1910–1955), Shields headed the international Baptist Bible Union for seven years [1923–1930]; edited a newspaper [*Gospel Witness*] which reached 30,000 subscribers in sixty different countries; served on the Board of Managers of McMaster University; established his own denomination; founded the Toronto Baptist Seminary and the Canadian Protestant League; held the office of acting president and, of late, was chairman of the Board of Governors of Des Moines (Iowa) University; wrote the doctrinal statement of the International Council of Christian Churches; helped to organize the Latin American Alliance of Christian Churches; and, late in life, was elected president of the Canadian Council of Evangelical Churches.[9]

In addition, Shields played a significant and central role in splitting the Ontario and Quebec Baptists in the late 1920s into warring fundamentalist and non-fundamentalist fashions. The Jarvis Street minister was also an important agent in bringing about a similar division among Western Baptists – both in British Columbia and the Prairie provinces. In Central Canada and the West, Shields and his supporters in the 1920s, in particular, focused their fundamentalist critique on the so-called modernism of McMaster University and Brandon College – the two influential Baptist institutions of higher learning located outside of the Maritimes.[10] According to Shields, both at McMaster and Brandon, "nearly every principle of evangelical religion" has been "trampled under foot" by the convention Baptist disciples of modernism.[11] Shields must have agreed with the "modernist" *Christian Century* description of the huge "paradigm" gap dividing fundamentalists from modernists in the 1920s and 1930s:

The differences between Fundamentalism and Modernism are not mere surface differences which can be amiably waved aside or disregarded, but they are foundation differences, amounting to their radical dissimilarity almost to the differences between two distinct religions ... Two world-views, two moral ideals, two sets of personal attitudes have clashed, and it is a case of ostrich-like intelligence blindly to deny and evade the searching and serious character of the issue. Christianity, according to Fundamentalism, is one religion, Christianity, according to Modernism, is another religion.[12]

In one of the most balanced studies of Shields and the Canadian Baptists it has been argued persuasively that "Stripped of combative hyperbole and unscrupulous tactics, the message Shields desired to communicate was a valid one."[13] As far as Ms Lee Ann Purchase is concerned, Shields:

recognized the dangers inherent in the new [Biblical] criticism, the tendency to carry the doctrine of progressive revelation too far, resulting in an anthropocentric religion with self the only arbiter of truth. He echoed the sentiments of his forerunners in the battle. In 1884, John Harvard Castle [the American-born minister of Jarvis Street Baptist Church] admitted to a fear "that the methodology of the higher criticism threatened to become an end in itself, in effect a secular theology shaped exclusively by humanistic and scientific calculations and completely devoid of spirituality."[14]

Ms Purchase goes on to argue that:

Shields was convinced of the faith-destroying powers of the higher criticism and of his commission to combat with all he had. The tragedy is that the validity of his concerns was overshadowed by an enormous ego and a frequent inability to "speak the truth in love." As he decried the "move to substitute for Christianity a mere system of ethics," Shields was guilty of an equally undesirable antinomianism "that ignored the basic virtues of honesty, truth and courtesy."[15]

There was a yet more profound tragedy in the Shields' triggered fundamentalist-modernist controversy that shattered the Baptist Church in Central Canada and the West into bitter, often un-Christ-like warring factions in the 1920s. The bitter religious war "left the Baptist denomination in Canada ... exhausted"[16] and virtually destroyed whatever remained of the prophetic voice of the Canadian Baptists. Since 1927 to 1930, the period of the schism in both Central Canada and the West, Canadian Baptists have become increasingly irrelevant, defensive, and ignorant of their richly textured historical and theological heritage. Each side of the struggle was obsessed with emphasizing its separateness, distinctiveness, and intrinsic spiritual superiority. It may be argued that the ensuing rigidities stifled and distorted the Christian gospel and channeled religious thought back over well-worn paths, thus discouraging the truly daring, the venturesome, and those who might have spoken with prophetic voices and revitalized insight.

D espite his flaws, T.T. Shields towered above most of his Canadian Baptist and Protestant contemporaries. In the early fall of 1987, during my tenure as the Winthrop Pickard Bell Professor of Maritime Studies at Mount Allison University, I decided to try to discover why Shields had had so little impact on Maritime religious life in general and the Baptist denomination in particular during the 1920s and 1930s. In "Fundamentalism, Modernism and the Maritime Baptists in the 1920s and 1930s"[17] – my first Bell Lecture given on 29 September 1987 – I argued implicitly that one of the reasons why the Maritime Baptists had not emulated their Central and Western co-religionists in experiencing a serious schism in the interwar years was that T.T. Shields had not been able to influence events in the region. Maritime Baptists, I contended, "could not really empathize with the main North American Fundamentalist or Modernist propagandists because they perceived religion in a radically different manner."[18] And, as a result, Shields and his handful of Maritime supporters had discovered in the late 1920s and early 1930s that their "Manichean theological" message failed to strike a responsive chord with Maritime Baptists.

I was not particularly satisfied with all aspects of this explanation because I realized how persistent an advocate of fundamentalism Shields had been in other regions of Canada and in the United States. How hard had Shields actually tried to reshape the religious contours of Maritime religious life in the 1920s and 1930s? I began trying to answer this question, as well as fill in a number of holes in my "Fundamentalism" paper, in late October 1987. The following dozen or so pages are the product of that research. I had initially intended this work to become my second Bell Lecture, but the subject proved to be something of a dry hole, and I later had to find another topic for the lecture.

T he first mention of Maritime Baptists to be found in the pages
of the *Gospel Witness* occurred on 6 August 1925. This was a little
more than three years after T.T. Shields had published the first issue
of his new fundamentalist and Baptist publication. In a brief article
entitled "The Pastor Visits Nova Scotia," it was reported that Shields
had been invited to speak at the "two great evening meetings" of
"the Baptist Laymen's Fundamentalist league of the Maritime Provinces," to be held on 12 and 13 August. Shields had apparently been
informed that "Modernism is making tremendous strides in the Maritime Provinces; and that the laymen have felt led of the Lord to
band themselves together to contend earnestly for the faith." The
Truro conference was to be "the first Fundamentalist conference held
in the Maritime Provinces" and it was to be Shields first visit to the
region. Gertrude Palmer is, consequently, not accurate in contending
that Shields first met J.J. Sidey in Halifax in 1923, "the beginning of
a fellowship which was to last down through the years."[19]

On 20 August 1925 Shields wrote an editorial in the *Gospel Witness*
entitled "The Editor in the Maritime Provinces." Shields noted that
the Truro conference had taken place in the Immanuel Baptist
Church and that the representation "especially from Prince Edward
Island" (led by Sidey and Daggett) was quite encouraging. Shields
had spoken Tuesday, Wednesday, and Thursday evenings and also
participated "in some of the conferences during the day." Shields
wrote that he had been "greatly impressed with the sanity and mod-
eration of many of the brethren who gathered. There was one brother
from PEI [J.B. Daggett?] who told of the necessity he and his wife
felt of discussing these matters privately and not in the presence of
their children; for they did not want their children to lose all respect
for the Church of Christ." The pastor of the Jarvis Street Baptist
Church also reported that the Reverend J.B. Daggett, of Tryon, PEI,
was elected the interim president of the new "Maritime Provinces
Christian Fundamentals Association." (No mention, it should be
pointed out, was made of Sidey.) There was, moreover, a clear
"understanding ... that at an early date another conference would
be held in P.E.I." Shields then went on:

The story some of these brethren had to tell was really pathetic. There were
some brethren whose churches had been absorbed in the United Church
under modernist controls and with only a modernist message. They felt it

was impossible for them longer to continue in fellowship with this organization, and yet some of them, from their observation of some Baptists, were almost as much afraid of a Baptist Church. We have said it before; we say it again: Oh that the Baptists of Canada would recognize that never in all the long history of this country were they faced with such an opportunity as faces us at present!

As far as Shields was concerned, if the Canadian Baptists were to enthusiastically preach "a plain uncompromised gospel ... in the power of the Holy Ghost" Baptist "numbers would increase by multiplied thousands." Realizing for the first time the numerical significance of the Maritime Convention Baptists within the larger context of Canadian religious life, Shields became determined to make the Maritime Baptists "better known in Ontario and Quebec."

After the Truro conference, the Reverend J.B. Daggett had accompanied Shields on the train as far as Sackville, New Brunswick. Shields maintained that he was "privileged to enjoy the fellowship of Daggett and had asked the Island minister to write an article or two about "the Baptist situation in the Maritime Provinces." This Daggett had promised to do. His article entitled "Baptists In The Maritime Provinces" followed the Shields' editorial in the 20 August 1925 issue of the *Gospel Witness*. Daggett's article was surprisingly weak in its historical analysis, but it was also disturbingly frank in its examination of the contemporary religious situation in the Maritimes. After contending that the Maritimes had been originally "settled by immigrants from the United Kingdom, the major part coming from England," the Grand Manan native maintained that they had, after the Revolution, been "added to by the United Empire Loyalists ... the great majority [of whom] were adherents to the Church of England." Eventually, according to Daggett, as the nineteenth century unfolded: "A few men and women moved by the Holy Ghost began breaking away from the established order; and soon a mighty revival of New Testament religion was sweeping over the land; with the result that Baptist Churches were established east, west, north and south, in every town, city and hamlet. They grew up beside our great rivers, and in our forest settlements; and in a comparatively short time, the Baptists were the largest Protestant body in the provinces." It seemed as though Daggett were viewing all nineteenth-century Maritime Baptist growth through the prism of his experience in Grand Manan where, in the mid-nineteenth century, the Anglican hegemony over the Island had been shattered by a Free Christian Baptist revival led by the remarkable Reverend Joshua Barnes.[20]

"Through the years," Daggett went on, "the Baptists have been able to hold a strong position and have had a larger influence upon public life." Due to the "might" of "the Lord Jehovah," Maritime Baptists had been given a "goodly heritage" and had been established "in a large place." Then, during "the past few years," the Baptists were faced with two difficult problems. First, there had been a "large exodus" of Baptists to the United States and to Central Canada and the West and, consequently, Daggett lamented, "many of our churches have been much weakened." He hoped, however, "that a good number of those who have gone from us will return better and wiser from having tried other pastures." Second, and of far greater consequence than the "exodus," was the fact that so many convention Baptists were abandoning traditional evangelical Baptistic principles, especially what Daggett referred to as the "Baptist interpretation of the Word." According to Daggett, key convention "leaders" were at the helm of this movement. In particular, Daggett zeroed in on what he regarded as the vociferous anti-Christian modernist statements of the Reverend Ross Eaton, minister of the prestigious First United Baptist Church in Charlottetown. He created the impression that Eaton was only one of many liberal Baptist ministers in the Maritimes. Daggett reported Eaton had stated publicly that, as far as the Trinity was concerned, "he could not accept the view of one in three and three in one" and that the orthodox view of the Trinity "did not commend itself to his way of thinking, and his judgment could not accept it." Later, at yet another quarterly association meeting, Eaton had rubbed more modernist theological salt into the festering fundamentalist wounds. In a sermon on the topic "God," the Charlottetown minister had proudly declared that "the Bible was [merely] an historical compilation of sixty-six books." Daggett went on paraphrasing the minister: "Its early books were made up largely of oriental imagery; it was not complete; there should be some system by which we should be adding to the Bible: there should be a New Acts of the Apostles. He [Eaton] quoted from H.G. Wells and referred to him as 'our good friend.'"

This positive reference to Wells infuriated Daggett and his fundamentalist friends, who were convinced that Wells had, in his *History of the World*, "definitely question[ed] the Deity of Jesus by subtle insinuation."

Eaton, it was reported, had not only publicly attacked the Bible and the Trinity on occasion but also at "our recent Association" meeting had questioned the validity of Christian missions and had espoused the cause of the Social Gospel. Eaton presented "what he was pleased to call a new conception of Christ, and a new conception of our missionary work and methods. No longer can we go to the heathen world to save them from hell; it does not appeal to-day. Our mission is to help these people to live now, better homes, better food, better physical conditions, education, etc., etc., then these people will naturally turn to Christianity." The incensed Daggett could only ask the question – can such a person really be "a friend of Baptists?" – and then answer it immediately: Eaton, like Wells, was really "no friend of Jesus" and certainly "not a friend of the old-time Baptists."

Daggett declared that "if Mr. Eaton is right, then many of us have been and are wrong ... I can see no meeting or common ground for us." He asserted that due to the growing influence of Eaton and his friends there were, throughout the three Maritime provinces, "signs of a great spiritual drought: the heavens are being shut up; there are a few scattered showers of blessing; but the early and latter rains are not upon the land; in some places the evening dew has well nigh failed." The aroused and angry Daggett denounced "horse-racing, dancing, card-playing, theatre-going, pleasure-loving" Baptists who were "increasing in city and country ... The old gospel we hear has lost its power, we must have something new. It is not the gospel that has lost its power, it is the pulpit and the preacher. Trained singers and Sunday operas cannot take the place of the message: 'Behold the Lamb of God, which taketh away the sin of the world.' 'Feed my sheep' was and is still our Lord's message. We have some hungry flocks in this country today."

It was Daggett's contention that many of the real problems confronting the convention could be traced directly to the new "scholarship" propagated by those "young fellows who may have a degree but who has yet to cut his eye-teeth in the world's university of real experience." "Some of the world's greatest men," Daggett argued, "have never seen college walls, except on the outside; some of our college professors couldn't run a wheelbarrow without someone to steady it for them." Daggett, despite his brief sojourns at Colby College and the University of New Brunswick, had little use for higher education; he considered it to be basically antagonistic to the simple Christian faith.

On 24 September 1925 the *Gospel Witness* published Daggett's second article, entitled "Good News From Down by the Sea." It described the annual convention of the Maritime Baptists held at Acadia University from 26-30 August. Daggett had been particularly impressed with what he described as "the splendid spiritual tone that was maintained throughout the Convention," despite an offensive unleashed by so-called modernist ministers attending the Wolfville meetings. He proudly contrasted the daily "prayer and experience meetings" held in the college chapel with the blatantly modernist sermon entitled "The Religion of the Future" preached by the Reverend A.L. Huddleston, minister of the prestigious First Baptist Church, Halifax. According to Daggett, Huddleston's sermon, which had been primarily concerned with praising the Reverend Harry Fosdick, the nemesis of America fundamentalism, "fell like the proverbial water on the duck's back. It ran off and left no mark." Daggett estimated that "Ninety-five percent of Maritime Baptists are true to the message of the Book, and to the faith of the fathers." He was therefore relieved to report:

At present there is a spirit of good nature and tolerance, coupled with the hope that these brethren will soon find themselves and get back to real vital experience and to the old message. During Convention we heard apologies made for them. "They are young and immature." "They are too soon from the schools." "They have shot their bolt, and nobody pays any attention to them." If it is true that they are too soon from the schools, and it takes a man from five to ten years, in the best of his life to shed his coat, and get rid of what he got in the schools, the sooner some of these schools are closed up the better, or we ought to have a house-cleaning and that without delay, and get rid of some of the immature professors who are turning out such immature products.

What Daggett was proposing on the pages of the *Gospel Witness* was that there be a thorough housecleaning at Acadia University. Once this were done, he was certain that the forces of modernity would be kept in careful check by the strong fundamentalist and conservative evangelical elements in the convention. If, however, such change from the top down did not take place immediately in the convention, he warned that "there is a spirit which is ready to say 'Hitherto shalt thou come but no further' and is even now prepared to fight for the faith once for all delivered to the Saints." He emphasized that the vast majority of convention Baptists in the Maritimes did not believe that "the religion of the future is the Fosdick type; they still believe in the Deity of Christ, in His miracles, in His atonement, His resurrection, ascension and intercession. Oh yes and His return." Daggett then concluded with a powerful fundamentalist statement of certainty: "If the Maritime Baptists were called upon to-day to take their stand, they are ready to exalt the Deity of Christ about His humanity. They are ready to declare that His atoning death upon the cross eclipsed His feeding of the multitude, and cleansing of the lepers; that His blood applied to the hearts of men is infinitely more potent in saving men than the most perfect environment. If the test should come, the voice of the Baptists by the sea would be as the voice of many waters. They know how to wield shield and buckler." Daggett was convinced there was a fundamentalistic mainstream in the convention, and that "Like a mighty river it flows quietly, but it is deep and powerful."

The September 1925 article was Daggett's last in the *Gospel Witness*, and the penultimate discussion of the Maritime Baptists found in Shields' publication in the interwar years. On 20 May 1926, Shields reported he had been informed that the Reverend Huddleston was being considered for the pastorate of the Park Baptist Church, Brantford. In response, Shields reprinted Daggett's 24 September 1925 denunciation of Huddleston and concluded his two-paragraph story with this question: "We wonder if the Park Church, so long noted for its orthodoxy, has so declined from the faith that it will willingly call to its pulpit one who is in accord with Dr. Harry Emerson Fosdick?" Huddleston, it should be noted, never left Nova Scotia.

A question that immediately comes to mind is why Shields so assiduously avoided any mention of the Maritime Baptists in the 1926–39 period. It might seem that he had lost faith in their ability to distinguish clearly between fundamentalism and modernism, since there was no Maritime secessionist movement in the late 1920s to match his Central Canadian schism. The available evidence, however, suggests that in the post-1926 period Shields was, as might have been expected, preoccupied with evolving events in Ontario, Quebec, and the West, as well as in the United States. He was, it should be remembered, actively involved in the fundamentalist Baptist takeover of Des Moines University, Iowa, in May 1927.[21] Unable to put things right at McMaster University, Shields had enthusiastically turned to the task of transforming Des Moines into what

McMaster had refused to be – "a great Christian institution of higher learning ... absolutely free from the taint of modernism."[22]

But, within two years, the Des Moines experiment had proven to be an embarrassing failure; a student revolt and a bitter American reaction against the Anglophile Shields led to the closing of the university in 1929. As chairman of the board of Des Moines University, Shields had barred the popular fraternities and sororities from campus and, moreover, had developed a very effective student and faculty spy network to discover who on campus was loyal or disloyal to the fundamentalist cause and to him. It is therefore not surprising that from 1927–29 Shields was indifferent to the Maritimes. Then, in 1931, for theological and personal reasons, most of Shields' followers from the late 1920s left his Union of Regular Baptist Churches of Ontario and Quebec. In 1933 they formed the new Fellowship of Independent Baptist Churches of Canada. Because of this bitter separation, one that had been brewing for some time, Shields was forced to concentrate his attention on Central Canada.

When J.B. Daggett and the Reverend J.J. Sidey, his close friend and confidante, led a fundamentalist Baptist schismatic movement out of the Maritime convention in 1933 and 1934, they chose to develop closer ties with Shields' fellowship opponents than with Shields himself. It seems that the ardent premillennialism of Daggett and Sidey found a sympathetic counterpart among the Central Canadian fellowship Baptists, whose uncompromising premillennialism was a key reason for their having quit the Shields' union. Even though Shields was a moderate premillennialist in the 1920s, he never considered premillennialism to be a crucially important tenet of fundamentalism.[23] This seemed to be the excuse that some of the fellowship Baptist leaders were looking for in order to justify their break from Shields, whose dictatorial methods were resented by an emerging ministerial élite.

As recently as the 1980s, Sidey's disciples in the Kingston area of Nova Scotia still resent the fact that Shields offered Sidey and Daggett no help in the 1930s, at a time when outside assistance was desperately needed. "If only Shields had helped us out in 1933 and 1934 and 1935" one of them maintained in August 1987, "things would have been so different for the true Baptist cause."[24] Things might have been radically different if Shields had been enthusiastically and directly involved in the Maritime fundamentalist Baptist schism in the 1930s. On the other hand, the evidence is very persuasive that things would not have been much different after all. Maritimers in the 1920s and 1930s did not like outsiders telling them what to do, especially Torontonians. They still do not and it should not be forgotten, furthermore, that convention Baptists always possessed a strong sense of regional identity. They still do – although, unfortunately, it is weakening.

While the above sheds some light on a hitherto little discussed relationship, I had a hunch – nothing more than a hunch – that there was something more to the relationship. But I needed more – I needed evidence, especially some correspondence between Shields and one of the key Maritime players. I knew from Robert Delnay's doctoral dissertation, "A History of the Baptist Bible Union," done at Dallas Theological Seminary, that there were some very valuable Shields letters in the Jarvis Street Baptist Church. But it was impossible to ascertain from the dissertation and from Delnay's articles based on it how extensive the Shields correspondence actually was.[25] I needed to get into the Jarvis Street Baptist Church Archives, but I knew that a number of scholars had failed in the past to obtain such permission. Walter Ellis, for instance, had been unsuccessful in his bid to see the Shields Papers, though he had nevertheless written a fine PHD dissertation, "Social and Religious Factors in the Fundamentalist-Modernist Schism ... 1895-1934" at the University of Pittsburgh in 1974. How was I to open the door that had been closed to everyone except Delnay, an enthusiastic disciple of Shields? In early December 1987, on my return to Kingston, Ontario, I learned that the Reverend Mark Parent, minister of the First Baptist Church, Kingston, had been given permission to look at the Shields Papers provided that he organize them for the Jarvis Street Baptist Church. Reverend Parent was beginning a PHD thesis at McGill University on the Christology of T.T. Shields. Parent, who was my minister, asked me to accompany him to Jarvis Street to advise him on his project. Though a convention Baptist minister, Parent had used his considerable persuasive powers to convince the Jarvis Street deacons and minister that he should be free to view the Shields material. Mark Parent and I discovered scores of letters relating to the Maritimes – letters that covered the 1924 to 1948 period. The material found in the Shields Papers put a rather different perspective on the fundamentalist-modernist controversy in the Maritimes in the late 1920s and 1930s. The new Shields papers underscored two very important revisions to my published and unpublished work. First, T.T. Shields was far more involved in the Kingston Parsonage Case of 1934 than I had ever realized. Second, Shields regarded Daggett and not Sidey as the key fundamentalist leader in the Maritimes.

In early 1924 Daggett became a delighted subscriber to the *Gospel Witness*. On receiving his first issue on 12 February 1924, Daggett wrote to Shields from Tryon, Prince Edward Island.[26] In this, his first letter to Shields, Daggett attacked the Reverend Ross Eaton, minister of the First United Baptist Church, Charlottetown, calling him "a modernist and an advocate of the *"Christian ? Century."* The Tryon minister then concluded: "The situation is rapidly becoming serious with us in our Maritime Convention. The modernists are slowly getting control. They have been fairly quiet and subtle in the past but they are now moving out in the open. It looks as though we have stormy days ahead." On 6 March 1924 Shields penned a brief reply to Daggett, asking him to become a member of the Baptist Bible Union. In his letter Shields also agreed that modernism was "spreading like a plague everywhere." "Nothing short of a great spiritual awakening," he went on, "will stay its progress." He stressed, however, that all true believers were "under obligation to stand against it at all costs."

Encouraged by Shields' reply, Daggett wrote yet another letter to the Toronto fundamentalist on March 14. Once again Daggett denounced the "current of modernism" flowing through the Maritime Baptist Convention from its "badly tainted" source at Acadia University. He denounced the *Maritime Baptist* as being in the hands of those who believed in "the need of a revised gospel." Daggett was concerned that the forces of modernism had in fact succeeded in putting the advocates of Christian orthodoxy on the defensive. And he asked Shields to do everything in his power to "organize a Bible Union down here by the sea at an early date ... I do not feel I am in a position to lead," Daggett confessed, "but will be a very faithful follower." Daggett was obviously looking to Shields to lead a fundamentalist counter-offensive in the Maritimes.

On 25 March 1925 Shields informed Daggett that he was just too busy to come immediately to the Maritimes – an area of Canada he had *"never"* before visited.[27] He again urged Daggett to try to "organize a Bible Union," saying that once this was done he promised to come "sometime in the future." Shields therefore felt obligated to attend the Truro Fundamentalist Conference that took place the first week of August, a conference organized to a great extent by Daggett.

It was in Truro that Shields first met Sidey, whom the Toronto minister regarded as being Daggett's second-lieutenant, at best. Sidey's first letter to Shields was written on 18 August 1925. It was an obsequious note in which Sidey underscored the "wonderful opportunity" Shields had "at Jarvis St." It is clear from Shields' correspondence with the Reverend R.W. Bennett, minister of Emmanuel Baptist Church, Truro, that in August 1925 Shields regarded Daggett and Bennett to be the principal fundamentalist leaders in the Maritimes. Sidey had been unceremoniously pushed by Shields to the periphery of the Maritime fundamentalist movement.

Shields seemed to have been delighted with Daggett's 20 August article in the *Gospel Witness*. He reported to the Reverend R.W. Bennett on 1 September 1925: "I sent a copy of the issue which I enclose, containing Daggett's article, to every Baptist pastor, to every church clerk, and to every superintendent in the Maritime Provinces. I thought it might help to stir something up and awaken the people to the perils of the hour." The Daggett article certainly did "stir something up" in the Maritimes, especially at the convention of the United Maritime Baptists in Wolfville from 26-30 August. On 3 September Daggett wrote to his Toronto chief about the reception given the controversial *Gospel Witness* article. According to Daggett, the convention leaders "were not long in getting after me; but they were very careful and diplomatic and assumed a very paternal air and sort of advised me to wash my face, comb my hair and like a good boy go sit in a corner. But I did not feel inclined to do that," Daggett went on, "and in very plain language stated my position and gave them to understand that I was going to stay with the colours." He informed Shields that there were reports at the convention "that you were leading the denomination straight for the rocks" but, despite this nasty propaganda, Daggett was "satisfied our people are 90 per cent sound." Instead of attacking the convention leadership Daggett had thought it "best to allow things to go on as they were for this session and during the year to get lined up for the battle."

On 4 September Daggett sent his second article to the *Gospel Witness*; it was published later in the month. Daggett was not, it should be pointed out, the only Maritime Baptist writing to Shields about the August convention. On 9 September the Reverend R.W. Bennett had sent a long letter to Shields. Interestingly, none was sent by Sidey, who was still obviously a minor actor on the fundamentalist stage. The Bennett letter provides fascinating insight into how one pro-Shields Maritime Baptist minister in 1925 was actually treated by key convention leaders.

At the beginning of his letter Bennett observed: "About the convention, well, I am sick of it. It is true that modernism was not to the fore. Perhaps it would be much nearer the truth to say that it WAS KEPT IN THE BACKGROUND. It tried to lift its miserable head but dare not. All day on the Thursday of the convention we were on a powder box, we all felt it, it was only the prayers of Godly men that prevented a terrible explosion." Because of the 20 August *Gospel Witness*, which had been read, it seemed, by every convention delegate, Bennett "at once found myself in an ice box. There were few of my old friends," he noted sadly, "who would give me more than a nod, or HOW DO YOU DO? A bunch of modernists were out in deep conversation and reading something. I happened to be standing on the steps near by when one of them Dr. Spidell [sic] saw me and said 'Here he is now' and then addressing me said 'I see that Dr. Shields is speaking a good word for you in his paper.'" A furious Bennett retorted "I am flattered. It is more than could be expected from a mere stranger." Spidle, the dean of theology at Acadia then denounced Bennett for "letting [Shields] into my church," and the minister of Emmanual Baptist Church counter-attacked that he was "capable of running my own Church, that this was my business and that they were to keep their hands off." Then the Reverend Huddleston, the articulate anti-fundamentalist minister of First Baptist Church, Halifax, joined in the fray by slyly suggesting that he had always thought that Bennett had been "a modernist." Bennett was furious at these verbal jabs and felt compelled to tell Spidle, Huddleston, and their allies that "I was a modernist with a big M and the Book that they were assuming to correct was a modern book, in fact the most modern book in the world, it met modern needs, but that henceforth they must consider me also a confirmed and unbending Fundimentalist [sic] ... Thus the line is drawn," Bennett proudly observed. He also reported to Shields that "Poor Dagget got it too, but believe me he is a match for them."

Bennett was both surprised and delighted to discover that "THERE ARE SCORES OF OUR MEN WHO HAVE NOT BOWED THE KNEE TO MOD-

ERNISM ... Scores of them are true to the OLD BOOK." If "the fight had been started" on the convention floor, he predicted that "the worshipers of modernism would have been swept into the sea." Even at Acadia there were "only a few of the professors that are real bad"; and President Patterson was considered to be "reasonably safe." Dr H.T. DeWolfe, professor of New Testament and language was, according to Bennett "our key man when the time comes ... In his devotional addresses" to the convention he was: "ABSOLUTELY SAFE. He flayed modernism without being personal. He stood for Inspiration and all we stand for that. But he told me that he hates your methods of attack. He thinks that your saying that Fosdick and others have never seen the FACE OF CHRIST was terrible. I am sure that he does not like you. He told me that Dear old Dr. Keirsted [sic] left his classes [at McMaster] and went out West lecturing for the Fundimentalist [sic] movement without even mentioning it to the President."

In his description of DeWolfe's reaction to Shields, Bennett had, almost despite himself, put his finger on the essential differences between the fundamentalist mind-set and that of the conservative evangelical. Moreover, he had pointed out the closed-mindedness of Shields and the open-mindedness of DeWolfe, whose two evangelical theologies were obviously in conflict.

After denouncing, as had Daggett in his September *Gospel Witness* article, the Reverend Ross Eaton's "poor oration – poorly recited PUNK ... MODERNISM," Bennett described in an evocative manner the "most sacred Prayer Meeting I have attended for years." The meeting took place early Sunday morning: "The Lord took it out of our hands and greatly blessed us. There was not a modernist present. He could not have lived in it. Men and women, Ministers and all of us were in tears. Old men said that nothing more blessed had come to them for many a day."

It is noteworthy that Bennett added a brief PS to his letter. "I guess this is personal and not yet for publication. The time is not ripe." The time would never be ripe for the rather frustrated Bennett, who later in 1925 resolved to leave Nova Scotia to accept a call to the Carew Street Baptist Church, Springfield, Massachusetts. Before he left Nova Scotia, Bennett denounced "our fundamental brethren ... of small intellect" who criticized him for not preaching a strong premillennial gospel. Bennett complained to Shields that as a result of this internecine warfare "the fundamental cause is greatly suffering" and "The Modernists are making capital out of these weaknesses." "I wish," Bennett moaned, "we could capture a little brain for the cause."[28] Once again Bennett had perceptively observed a key weakness in the Maritime fundamentalist movement: the tension that existed between the premillennialists and the non-premillennialists, between a borrowed non-Maritime Baptist eschatology and the Maritime Baptist mainstream eschatology.

While Bennett was making plans to leave Truro in late 1925, Daggett was experiencing firsthand a great deal of strong negative reaction, especially to his second *Gospel Witness* article. "The fat is in the fire" he reported in a letter to Shields on 10 October 1925. "My two letters in the 'Witness' have stirred things up in good shape." Because of this and because of "the very wet season," the planned Second Fundamentalist Conference had to be cancelled. Instead of organizing the conference, Daggett resolved to continue attacking his modernist nemesis, Ross Eaton, whom he described as "an awful dodger, a typical modernist." Daggett had informed Eaton that the fundamentalist critique would stop only when the Charlottetown minister accepted the following fundamentals of the faith:

That the Bible (Old and New Testament) is the inspired infallible word of God involving
1 The virgin Birth of Jesus
2 Jesus as God the Son
3 His life as an example for believers
4 His death as atonement for sin
5 His Resurrection in the body of flesh
6 His ascension and intercession
7 His return
8 The God Head
   a God the Father
   b God the Son
   c God the Holy Ghost
9 The Holy Spirit as the one and only head of the Church indwelling and abiding as a person (not a Personality) in the hearts of believers and the Church.

In concluding his letter to Shields, Daggett proudly but perhaps also somewhat plaintively declared "I am the bad man down here just now." Then, bowing to pressure from a growing number of critics in his own congregation, Daggett, like Bennett, decided to leave his church. In 1926 Daggett resigned as minister of the Tryon PEI Baptist Church to accept a call to the Kingston-Melvern Square United Baptist pastorate in Nova Scotia.

When Daggett settled into his Nova Scotia pastorate he seemed less and less interested in cultivating his relationship with Shields. Perhaps the 1927 expulsion of Shields and his supporters from the Ontario and Quebec Convention persuaded Daggett that it would be unwise to wave with too much enthusiasm the Shields fundamentalist banner in the Maritimes. There is also some evidence to suggest that both diabetes and the aftereffects of tuberculosis had, by the late 1920s, forced Daggett to give up some of his causes and to be far more careful about overextending himself.[29] With Bennett now in the United States and with Daggett somewhat incapacitated, J.J. Sidey thrust himself forward late in November 1926 as the leader of the fundamentalist cause in the Maritimes. From his Central Bedeque PEI Baptist base, Sidey informed Shields:

Have been following with interest your recent "fight for freedom" and wish to say that I am with you in my prayers, and if you need me, myself. Have been waiting the Lord's opening for doing something definite against Modernism, for years, and have tried several things here in the Maritimes, but with little success because of the particular situation here. Am here in the Baptist Church, and am doing what I find at hand, until the Lord opens the way to a larger fundamental opportunity of witness, for me. When I am wanted, I shall be found here on the job.[30]

Sidey feared that Shields would "probably ... not remember me, but I met you at Truro" in August 1925. (In his letter Sidey mistakenly referred to the conference having taken place in 1923). Shields never replied to Sidey's first letter; rather he had his secretary send Sidey a rather terse reply.

Not discouraged at all by this short note of 25 November 1926, Sidey penned a three-page letter to Shields on 16 August 1927. What Sidey did not realize was that, a year earlier, Shields had received an offer of a six-hundred-acre farm near Truro "as a site" for a Fundamentalist Bible College. Shields explained in a letter to William Aberhart, the future Social Credit premier of Alberta, that he certainly had "to hesitate to turn away from a thing of that sort, lest it should be the Lord's leading, and it may be that the Lord will, in this way, give us a foothold in Nova Scotia; and thus we shall have some bases from which to operate from coast to coast."[31] But Shields did not mention at this time the possibility of a Truro Bible school either to Sidey or to Daggett, probably because he wished to retain a firm control over any new fundamentalist institution to be established in the Maritimes.

In his 16 August 1927 letter Sidey felt it necessary to again introduce himself to Shields by associating himself with "my friend J.B. Daggett." Sidey emphasized the fact that since Daggett "has been quite poorly, and it looks as though his work is fast hastening to its close," that Sidey should not be regarded as the major spokesman for Shields' Campaign of Information in the Maritimes. As far as Sidey was concerned, only Shields could breathe life into the Maritime fundamentalist movement "from Toronto." Sidey was "convinced ... it is useless to try and do anything more from any center in the Maritimes." Then the Bedeque minister underscored his total dependence on Shields: "Personally I am convinced that I cannot do anything more in the Maritimes, but feel that if some of us were connected directly with your work in Jarvis Street, after a time, we might be in a better position to do something. At present I feel that I am wasting my time on a proposition that is getting nowhere." For Sidey, in 1927, there seemed to be very little fundamentalist potential in Prince Edward Island in particular and the Maritime provinces in general. The region was "exceedingly over-churched" and the existing churches, especially on the Island, were too rural in their orientation. "Being a city-bred man," Sidey complained yet again, "I feel that I am wasting my time." "The City Churches" he stressed "are so under the Control of the Machine that it is impossible to get into them, and if we did, they are comparatively small, which makes aggressive Fundamentalist work almost impossible."

Then Sidey finally got to the essential point of his letter: "Can I be of any use to you on your Seminary Faculty? Financially I would not be much of a burden," Sidey declared, "as I have private means, and could thus serve at much less cost than men absolutely dependent upon their salary." And if a position was not available in Toronto, Sidey indicated that he was willing to return to the United States to teach at Des Moines University. Here or in Toronto he knew he could serve the "Cause of Bible Truth."

Sidey's almost embarrassing offer to become involved with the Toronto minister in the "aggressive Work for the Lord" was not accepted. Instead Sidey would have to be satisfied with moving to the Kingston-Malvern Square United Baptist Pastorate and, along with Daggett, attempting to emulate Shields' schismatic movement in the Maritimes. Rejected by Shields, yet inspired by him, Sidey had resolved by 1930 to lead the Baptist fundamentalist movement in the Maritimes. Driven to bankruptcy by his ill-fated silver fox investments on the Island, Sidey had come to realize in early 1930 that perhaps he was not "wasting [his] time" after all in the Maritimes.

S oon after the founding of The Union of Regular Baptist Churches of Ontario and Quebec in 1927 by Shields and his followers, bitter divisions appeared in the new denomination. These divisions were triggered by Shields' autocratic style, as well as his sharp criticism of the premillennial Scofieldian emphasis of a growing number of his followers. By 1933 the so-called rebels had "organized" the Fellowship of Independent Baptist Churches of Canada. Shields would continue as president of the union until 1949 "when he was ousted from that office by persons who resented his dictatorial policies and who expressed lack of confidence in his leadership."[32] While confronting his own doctrinally based schismatic movement in Central Canada in the early 1930s, Shields had little time for the Maritimes. But he did have time to consider the merits of retaining the six-hundred-acre property near Truro, Nova Scotia. He finally asked Daggett, in the summer of 1931, to investigate the matter for him, and Daggett presented a very negative report. He described the property as being isolated, and "of no consequence" and "as a school centre impractical." There was also an important implicit message to Shields in Daggett's letter of 22 July 1931. There was already a fundamentalist Bible College in Nova Scotia, at Kingston, and one was enough in a region where modernism seemed to be gaining in strength.[33] Daggett eventually succeeded in persuading Shields that building a school on the Truro property was, as Shields later put it, "a fool's errand." "As soon as I heard that you had founded a school down there," Shields informed the relieved Daggett, "I reached the conclusion that that is what ought to be done."

Daggett was not satisfied with merely reporting in the summer of 1931 to Shields about the Truro property. He took the opportunity to make Shields aware of the general religious situation in the Maritimes. According to a rejuvenated Daggett: "The atmosphere is becoming somewhat electric between us and the powers which be. I am sending the *Maritime Baptist* and Headquarters our literature, but we are being ignored as though we were highwaymen. There is a very loud profession of orthodoxy, and much talk of Evangelism, and quietly the word is being spread abroad that any coming from us will never be ordained ... So far the Lord has given us very special favour. We are going straight to the line. If war breaks out we are piling up ammunition and keeping it dry."

Little use, however, was made of Daggett's dry "ammunition," even in 1934 when he, Sidey, and a handful of supporters, left the Maritime Baptist Convention in order to establish the Independent and Fundamentalist Baptist Churches. There is no available evidence to suggest that Shields was either directly or indirectly involved in this minor schism. This may help to explain why the so-called fundamentalist-modernist controversy among Maritime Baptists in the 1930s was unable to bolster the extraordinarily weak secession movement in the Baptist heartland of Canada.

Shields may not have been, in the least, involved in the evolving events of 1933 and 1934 in the Maritime Baptist Convention. The Toronto minister was, however, very much involved in the Kingston Parsonage Case of 1935. It is now clear that Shields directed key parts of the Kingston drama and then abruptly abandoned the Maritime fundamentalist cause when he realized that Daggett and Sidey were supporting what was – at least in the 1930s – a losing cause.

In late November 1934 an enraged Daggett, reacting violently against the "illegal and rascally" convention, asked Shields for advice concerning disputed church property. Daggett asked if Shields had any relevant material about a rumoured Ontario court decision concerning "Convention Church property."[34] In his reply, Shields admitted that he had "been unable to follow proceedings in the Maritime Convention" and that the case referred to by Daggett had been "rather a peculiar thing."[35] Shields could therefore not, in all conscience, encourage Daggett in any church property venture in the Maritimes. On 22 January 1935 Shields enlarged on his earlier letter. He included with his letter a copy of the *Ontario Law Reports, 1929* which contained "a report of the Hughson Street case." "The essence of the case," according to Shields, was "merely a maintenance of the status quo, of 'as you were'" with the pro-Shields group being "assessed with the costs." Shields advised Daggett that if he was going to fight any church property case in a court of law in Nova Scotia it was absolutely essential that he prepare the lawyers "brief for him, and to sit at the table during the court proceedings to prompt him at every point," because it was "impossible for him to understand the genius of a Baptist Church's independency."

Thirteen days before the Kingston Parsonage Case was to be heard in Kentville, Daggett sent an urgent letter to Shields requesting that he send immediately to Kingston Shirley Jackson Case's *Revelation* and *Jesus Through the Centuries*.[36] Daggett informed Shields that "one of our points of contention is that the Convention placed their seal and approval on ... Case ... by giving him the honourary degree." Unfortunately, Daggett could not obtain a copy of either book "in this country except in the hands of some prominent modernist."

Shields sent Daggett the one Case volume he possessed, *Jesus Through the Centuries*, as well as the 1859 edition of *The New Directory for Baptist Churches*, C.M. Spurgeon's special 1870 edition of *Thirty-two Articles of Christian Faith and Practice*, and the 1934 Ontario and Quebec Convention *Year Book*.

Daggett was delighted with these books. On 24 May, the day before the last day of the trial, Daggett reported to Shields: "We could not get a lawyer in either the Baptist fold or the United Church who was not tied up solidly to the Convention. We got two Anglicans, very fine, but they knew nothing of Baptist Doctrine and it was an awful job to drill it into them, and both Sidey and myself had to sit beside them every moment, and the worst of all, is that the Judge is a dyed in the wool Anglican. He seemed to be fair, but could not comprehend our position."

It had become clear to Daggett what the real purpose of the trial was: "Whether we get the property or not we have had a wonderful opportunity to lay base modernism and we think we did it very well indeed. The enemy is gnashing his teeth, and all the powers of Satan are arrayed against us." Daggett requested that Shields "Ask your people to pray for us that the Judge shall yet see the light."

Even before Shields received the letter, thus before his and his congregration's potential prayers were answered, Daggett could report in a letter written late on 25 May, after the final word had been said in the Kingston Parsonage Case, that "We may lose the properties but God has given us a wonderful victory, our position has been fully demonstrated." He went on:

Evidence which we could not get in before was admitted today. Evidently they thought the Judge was favourable to them and today they put on their big guns from the University in rebuttal and strange to say the Judge, in cross examination, admitted everything that he ruled out two days before. We had a mass of evidence and got it all in. Case's book was a bombshell; it made people gasp that anybody would write such things about the Christ. We have now demonstrated from their own mouths that the Convention and Acadia University is rotten to the core with modernism, and they are a sick outfit tonight. The Lord has answered prayer. They cannot go through the country shouting Liars anymore.

Encouraged by Shields' positive response to his reports on the case, and also spurred on by two close associates of Shields – Messrs Kent and Taylor – in August Daggett prepared a long article for the *Gospel Witness* dealing with "Dr. Spidle's evidence." The article was based upon the official court transcript, which had been "purchased from the court clerk." Expecting his devastating critique to be published immediately by Shields, Daggett ordered "a few hundred copies" of the publication.[37] This Daggett article, however, was never published nor was a much longer study by Daggett "tell[ing] the story" of what Sidey referred to on 5 November 1935 as "our ... church work and the trial that recently took place in the Supreme Court of Nova Scotia." In order to ensure that this second article was actually published in the *Gospel Witness*, Daggett was eager to travel to "Toronto with all the material we have." It was his and Sidey's contention that the Kingston Case would be of considerable interest to all Canadian Baptists.

Shields did not reply to Sidey's letter of 5 November. Rather his secretary informed Sidey that the *Gospel Witness* was still interested but only in a "somewhat concise" article. The secretary also stressed that Shields felt there was no good reason for Daggett to travel "such a distance" to Toronto.[38] On 17 January 1936 Daggett sent "the first instalment of copy re the recent trial over Church Property" to the *Gospel Witness*. On 30 January he wrote to Miss Violet Stoakley, Shields' secretary, asking what had happened to his "first instalment." Then on 15 May an agitated Sidey complained to Shields: "We are anxiously awaiting some report from you regarding the evidence of our trial. The people are getting very anxious, and we are having inquiries all over the country as to when it will be out."

The article was never published in the *Gospel Witness*. There is a plaintive quality in Sidey's letter of 7 April 1939 to Shields announcing the death of Daggett on 15 January 1939. Realizing that Daggett had visited with Shields on two separate occasions, in September 1936 and March 1938, Sidey wondered "what plans or arrangements he [Daggett] may have had with you for the publishing of the Trial material." Sidey went on:

I understand that he visited you last March in order to converse with you along that line. We are trying to get his affairs straightened out, and among other things I see that you still have in Toronto the original evidence of the Trial. I should be pleased if you would mail this to us at your convenience, and if we have anything of yours that was not returned at the time, we will try to look it up. If Mr. Daggett entered into any arrangements with you regarding the publication of the Trial material, and you will let us know what they were, we will see whether we can continue the program that he had mapped out or if it is beyond our means, we will let you know. On the other hand, he may not have had any arrangements with you, and if so we would like to know, so that we can get all matters pertaining to his activities clear in our minds.

In reply the somewhat embarrassed Shields explained to Sidey the four-year delay in publication. He had talked the matter over with Daggett "but after looking at it from all angles, it seemed to me that no good purpose would be served by doing so." "The expense," he noted, "would be very considerable, and it seemed to me it would be pretty nearly a waste of money."[39] What Shields was really saying was that the case had never been newsworthy even for the *Gospel Witness*. He might have had a high regard for Daggett but he had little real empathy for Maritime Religious culture and, moreover, he saw no effective way to use the Kingston Parsonage Case to strengthen the fundamentalist cause in Canada. Shields seemed to accept Daggett's 1936 contention that the Maritime provinces were "the hardest place spiritually" for fundamentalists "on the Continent." "The Baptist Convention," in particular, was "the most perfect machine, and is manipulated without mercy." It was Daggett's first-hand experience that "Any man who dares to make a protest, his days are numbered, and the boycott is simply perfect, right down to the local church. It is carried into every phase of business and social life. The United Church works in perfect harmony with the United Baptist Convention."[40]

It is clear that at least until Dagget's death in January 1939, T.T. Shields was regarded by both Daggett and Sidey as their fundamentalist chieftain. There is an almost obsequious quality in all of their letters to the Jarvis Street minister. They saw Shields not as an equal but as a superior being; for them he was, without question, the most important and influential Canadian fundamentalist. Their profound dependence upon Shields, it may be argued, weakened rather than strengthened the fundamentalist cause in the Maritime provinces. They looked longingly to Toronto for fundamentalist direction and leadership when they should have been coming to grips instead with the unique evangelical religious culture of the Maritimes. They might have thus succeeded in revitalizing the Maritime convention Baptists in the 1920s and 1930s rather than forcing most Maritime Baptists into a defensive posture, from which they have never really recovered.

Shields' remarkable success in splitting the central and western Baptists into warring ideological factions was always contrasted with the almost embarrassing failure of his brand of fundamentalism to make any significant inroads in the Maritimes during the 1920s and 1930s. "Only the Maritime provinces" he once bitterly complained to William Aberhart – the future Social Credit premier of Alberta – remained "untouched" by the "really wonderful ... work ... the Lord has wrought."[41] Even Daggett, a short time before his death, would have reluctantly agreed with this assessment. From the vantage-point of 1939 in Kingston, Nova Scotia, it certainly seemed that the so-called modernist convention had successfully pushed the Daggett-Sidey forces into the dark periphery of Maritime religious life. This consolidation of power by the convention leaders was, in part, even their critics had to admit, the result of their more perceptive reading of the historical past and their more sensitive response to the realities of contemporary Maritime life.

T.T. Shields' failure in the Maritime provinces in the 1920s and 1930s was not due to lack of interest in the region. Nor was it due to the absence of key local leaders, for both Daggett and Sidey were indeed very gifted men. There was a fundamental and structural difference between the Baptist culture of the region and that in existence elsewhere in Canada. What Martin Lloyd-Jones once called the "negatory and denunciatory"[42] gospel of fundamentalism did not strike a responsive chord in a region and within a denomination which had, beginning in the late eighteenth century, been committed "to a more experiential, Christ-centred rather than doctrine-centred faith."[43] Despite the economic chaos produced by the Depression of the 1930s, and despite the increasingly vulnerable status of most Maritime Baptists, they were revolted by the Manichean world-view of the fundamentalists and by their eagerness to displace New Testament Christian love and forgiveness with Old Testament judgment and vengeance. Maritime Baptists were also, it may be argued, almost despite themselves, rejecting yet another manifestation of Upper Canadian cultural imperialism.

I t was indeed fortuitous that I discovered in December 1987 in the Shields Papers located in the Jarvis Street Baptist Church over fifty letters dealing with the Maritime Baptists in the 1920s and 1930s. These letters compelled me to revise in two major respects my earlier assessment of "Fundamentalism, Modernism, and the Maritime Baptists" in the interwar years. First, I had underestimated the direct and indirect influence exerted by T.T. Shields on unfolding events and on the principal actors in the ongoing religious drama. Second, I had failed to realize that within the context of the 1920s and 1930s, J.B. Daggett was probably more important than J.J. Sidey in the Maritime fundamentalist movement. Gertrude A. Palmer's The Combatant had, for me and for others, been responsible for thrusting Sidey to centre stage at the expense of J.B. Daggett. Historians, of course, are always attempting to recreate the past, and their restructuring of what actually happened soon becomes historical truth and historical fact. This is what Palmer had done in her biography of Sidey; The Combatant was the prism through which I originally perceived the fundamentalist side of the modernist-fundamentalist controversy of the 1920s and 1930s. From my new vantage point in Sackville, New Brunswick, in May 1988, taking into account the relevant Shields Papers, I was beginning to see a rather different picture – a picture which, I am sure, will be altered when new primary material is discovered. I merely write in the Maritime sand and wait for the tide to wash the beach clean – in preparation for new interpretations and new insights – however flawed.

Notes

ONE

1 See, for example, the emphasis placed upon "social relevance" in the evaluation of applications for Canada Council and SSHRCC research grants. N. Jackson of the Canada Council Killam Research Fellowship Programme to G.A. Rawlyk, 4 August 1987. (Letter in possession of the author.)

2 See S.A. Marini, "New England Folk Religions 1770–1815: The Sectarian Impulse in Revolutionary Society" (PHD diss., Harvard University, 1978), 20.

3 Letter from H.H. Budd to Robert Wright, April 1986. (Letter in possession of Robert Wright, Millbrook, Ont.)

4 Reginald Bibby, *Fragmented Gods: The Poverty and Potential of Religion in Canada* (Toronto, 1987), 108.

5 Comment made by Professor Tom Vincent, of RMC at the Planters' Conference, Wolfville, Nova Scotia, 23 October 1987.

6 See, for example, my *New Light Letters and Songs* (Hantsport, 1983), 4–22.

7 For a discussion of the "neutrality thesis" see M. Armstrong, "Neutrality and Religion in Revolutionary Nova Scotia," *The New England Quarterly* 9 (March 1940): 50–62.

8 See, in particular, J.M. Bumsted, *Henry Alline* (Toronto, 1971), 78 and D.G. Bell, ed., *Newlight Baptist Journals of James Manning and James Innis* (Hantsport, 1984), xiii.

9 This is the central thesis of Gordon Stewart and George Rawlyk, *A People Highly Favoured of God: The Nova Scotia Yankees and the American Revolution* (Toronto, 1972).

10 Bell, *Newlight Baptist Journals*, xiii.

11 J. More, *The History of Queens County Nova Scotia* (Halifax, 1873), 162.

12 H. Alline, *Life and Journal* (Boston, 1806), 35.

13 See J. Davis, *Life and Times of the Late Rev. Harris Harding, Yarmouth, N.S.* (Charlottetown, 1866) 178.

14 Marini, "New England Folk Religions," 479.

15 This theme is developed by D.D. Bruce Jr, *And They All Sang Hallelujah, Plain-Folk Camp Meeting Religion 1800-1845* (Knoxville, 1975), 95. See also Nathan Hatch, *The Democratization of American Christianity* (New Haven, 1989).

16 H. Alline, *Hymns and Spiritual Songs* (Boston, 1786), i–ii.

17 Ibid., 153–4.

18 Ibid., 162.

19 Ibid., 182–3.

20 Ibid., 348–349.

21 I have attended one of these services and found it, without question, both memorable and moving. The service convinced me that I had, in my earlier work on Alline, underestimated the powerful impact that the Allinite oral tradition had on Maritime religious culture in the nineteenth *and* the twentieth centuries.

22 M. Armstrong, *The Great Awakening in Nova Scotia, 1776-1809* (Hartford, 1948), 92.

23 See G. Patterson, *Memoir of the Rev. James McGregor* (Philadelphia, 1859), 92.

24 Armstrong, *The Great Awakening*, 92.

25 See my *Ravished By The Spirit: Religious Revivals, Baptists, and Henry Alline* (Kingston and Montreal, 1984), 1–35.

26 J. Beverley and B. Moody, eds., *The Life and Journal of The Rev. Mr. Henry Alline* (Hantsport, 1982), 208–9.

27 Ibid., 210.

28 Ibid.

29 D.C. Harvey and C.B. Fergusson, eds., *The Diary of Simeon Perkins 1780-1789,* (Toronto, 1958), 2:177.

30 Ibid.

31 Public Archives of Nova Scotia (PANS), "Records of the Church of Jebogue in Yarmouth," 140.

32 A. Heimert, *Religion and the American Mind from the Great Awakening to the Revolution* (Cambridge, 1966), 169.

33 See G.A. Rawlyk, ed., *The Sermons of Henry Alline* (Hantsport, 1986), 17.

34 See ibid., 14–33.
35 See Armstrong *The Great Awakening in Nova Scotia*, 86.
36 Rawlyk, *New Light Letters and Songs*, 38–63.
37 See T.W. Smith, *History of the Methodist Church ... of Eastern British North America* (Halifax, 1877), 150–1; G. French, *Parsons and Politics* (Toronto, 1962), 33–9; N. Bangs, *The Life of the Rev. Freeborn Garrettson* (New York, 1830); R.D. Simpson, "Freeborn Garrettson: American Methodist Pioneer," (PHD diss., Drew Theological Seminary, 1954); G.A. Rawlyk, "Freeborn Garrettson," *Dictionary of Canadian Biography, 1821-1835*, 11 vols. (Toronto, 1987), 6:275–76.
38 See N. MacKinnon's important book, *This Unfriendly Soil: The Loyalist Experience in Nova Scotia 1783-1791* (Kingston and Montreal, 1985).
39 Gordon Wood, "Evangelical America and Early Mormonism," (paper presented to the fifteenth annual meeting of the Mormon History Association, May, 1980), 2. See also Hatch *The Democraticization of American Christianity*.
40 Acadia University Archives, J.M. Cramp, "History of the Maritime Baptists."
41 Wood, "Evangelical America," 7.
42 Ibid., 10.
43 Ibid., 12.
44 See my *New Light Letters and Songs*, (Hantsport, 1983), 37–63.
45 W.C. Barclay, *Early American Methodism, 1769-1844*, 2 vols. (New York, 1949), 1:171.
46 Smith, *History of the Methodist Church*, 193–4.
47 Quoted in Bangs, *Garrettson*, 154.
48 J.M. Buckley, *A History of Methodism in the United States*, 2 vols. (New York, 1897), 1:171.
49 Rawlyk, "Freeborn Garrettson," 275.
50 Quoted in Smith, *History of the Methodist Church*, 152.
51 Ibid.
52 Quoted in Rawlyk, "Freeborn Garrettson," 275.
53 Quoted in Bangs, *Garrettson*, 177.
54 Ibid, 172.
55 *Methodist Magazine* (1827), 172.
57 W.H. Williams, *The Garden of American Methodism: The Delmarva Peninsula, 1769-1820* (Wilmington, 1984), 32.
57 Ibid.
58 Ibid.
59 Quoted in ibid., 32.

60 United Church Archives (UCA), Toronto, "Freeborn Garrettson Journal."

61 Ibid.

62 Ibid.

63 R.D. Simpson, ed., *American Methodist Pioneer: The Life and Journals of the Rev. Freeborn Garrettson 1752-1827* (Rutland, 1984), 127.

64 Quoted in Smith, *History of the Methodist Church*, 166.

65 UCA "Freeborn Garrettson Journal."

66 Ibid.

67 Simpson, *American Methodist Pioneer*, 129–30.

68 Quoted in Bangs, *Garrettson*, 171.

69 Simpson, *American Methodist Pioneer*, 131.

70 Quoted in Barclay, *Early American Methodism*, 1:171.

71 Simpson, *American Methodist Pioneer*, 6.

72 Quoted in W.G. McLoughlin, *Revivals, Awakenings and Reform: An Essay on Religion and Social Change in America 1607-1977* (Chicago, 1978), 15.

73 Ibid., 15.

74 Ibid., 16.

75 Ibid., 17.

76 Quoted in ibid., 17; see also P. Worsley, *The Trumpet Shall Sound* (London, 1968).

77 PANS MG I, vol. 93(a), Bishop Charles Inglis to the Reverend J. Barley, 3 April 1799.

78 Ibid.

79 See the very important historiographical article by L.I. Sweet in his finely edited volume, *The Evangelical Tradition in America* (Macon, 1984), 37.

80 Victor Turner, *The Ritual Process: Structure and Anti-Structure* (Ithaca, 1979), 94–140.

81 See the critical review by Gordon Stewart in the *Journal* of the Canadian Church History Society, 28 (1986): 45–6.

82 George Marsden, *Fundamentalism and American Culture: The Shaping of Twentieth-Century Evangelicalism 1870-1925* (New York, 1980). See some of the very positive comments about the book on the back cover of the 1982 paperback edition.

83 Marsden, *Fundamentalism*, 229–30.

84 Ibid., 230.

85 See David Weale, "The Ministry of the Reverend Donald McDonald on Prince Edward Island 1826-1867: A Case Study Examination of the

Influence and Role of Religion within Colonial Society," (PHD diss., Queen's University, 1976), 107–16.

86 See my *Henry Alline: Selected Writings* (Mahwah, 1987), 52.

87 Alline, *Two Mites*, (Halifax, 1781), 124–5.

88 Ibid., 20–1.

89 Alline, *The Anti-Traditionalist* (Halifax, 1783), 65.

90 Rawlyk, *The Sermons of Henry Alline*, 108.

91 Ibid., 49.

92 Ibid., 60.

93 Ibid., 96–7.

94 Ibid., 97.

95 Ibid.

96 Ibid., 145.

97 Ibid., 108.

98 *Oberlin Evangelist*, January 21, 1846.

99 *United Baptist Year Book 1921, 112.*

100 *United Baptist Year Book, 1940, 154.*

101 *United Baptist Year Book, 1936, 153.*

102 See Weale, "The Ministry of the Reverend Donald MacDonald."

103 See, for example, Watson Kirkconnell to J.M.R. Beveridge, 4 March 1966, in the Kirkconnell Papers, Acadia University Archives.

104 Quoted in D.W. Frank, *Less Than Conquerors* (Grand Rapids, 1986), 277.

TWO

1 See R.N. Bellah et al., *Habits of the Heart: Individualism and Commitment in American Life* (Berkeley, 1985). Most of the material in this lecture is to be found in my "Fundamentalism, Modernism, and the Maritime Baptists in the 1920s and 1930s," *Acadiensis* 13 (Fall 1987): 3–33.

2 Ibid., 275.

3 S. Toulmin, *The Return to Cosmology: Postmodern Science and the Theology of Nature* (Berkeley, 1982), 228–29.

4 Bellah, *Habits of the Heart*, 283.

5 See ibid., 275–93.

6 Quoted in ibid., 176.

7 Ibid., 183.

8 David Bell, "All Things New: The Transformation of Maritime Baptist Historiography," *Nova Scotia Historical Review* 4, no. 2 (Spring 1984): 70.

9. See, for example, D.G. Bell, ed., *New Light Baptist Journals of James Manning and James Innis* (Hantsport, 1984); G.A. Rawlyk, ed., *The New Light Letters and Spiritual Songs* (Hantsport, 1983) and G.A. Rawlyk, *Ravished by the Spirit: Religious Revivals, Baptists and Henry Alline* (Kingston and Montreal, 1984); J.M. Bumsted, *Henry Alline, 1748-1784* (Toronto, 1971); M.W. Armstrong, *The Great Awakening in Nova Scotia, 1776-1809* (Hartford, 1948).

10 Murphy, "The Religious History of Atlantic Canada: The State of the Art," *Acadiensis* 15 no. 1 (Autumn 1985): 173.

11 Ernie Forbes, "Prohibition and the Social Gospel in Nova Scotia," *Acadiensis* 1 no. 1 (Autumn 1971): 11–36.

12 See Rawlyk, *Ravished by the Spirit*, 170–72.

13 See W. Ellis, "Social and Religious Factors in the Fundamentalist-Modernist Schisms Among Baptists in North America, 1895-1930," (PHD diss., University of Pittsburgh, 1974); M.B.R. Hill, "From Sect to Denomination in the Baptist Church in Canada," (PHD diss., State University of New York at Buffalo, 1971); G.H. Poucett, "A History of the Convention of Baptist Churches of British Columbia," (Master's thesis, Vancouver School of Theology, 1982); J.B. Richards, *Baptists in British Columbia* (Vancouver, 1976).

14 L.K. Tarr, *Shields of Canada* (Grand Rapids, 1967); C.A. Russell, "Thomas Todhunter Shields, Canadian Fundamentalist," *Foundations* 24 no. 1 (Winter 1981): 15–31.

15 Gertrude A. Palmer, *The Combatant* (Middleton, 1976). Palmer, author of this somewhat uncritical and superficial biography of Sidey, was one of his followers.

16 See, for example, *Maritime Baptist*, published in Kentville, for this period together with *The United Baptist Year Book* which was printed annually in Truro.

17 The biographical material is based upon Sidey's letter of 5 September 1934 to the editor of the *Middleton Outlook* and upon Sidey's testimony in the famous 1935 Kingston Baptist Parsonage Case. The *Outlook* letter is in the possession of Mrs George Moody, Wolfville, Nova Scotia. A copy of the official transcript of this trial is to be found in the Acadia University Archives (AUA). Hereafter, the transcript shall be referred to as Court Records. I have not yet been able to find the original transcript of the trial.

18 See Palmer, *The Combatant*, 25.

19 Ibid, 26.

20 Ibid., 27. I have a copy of Sidey's academic record at Garrett in my possession.

21 Court Records, AUA.

22 Ibid.

23 Quoted in Palmer, *The Combatant*, 32.

24 Court Records, AUA.

25 Quoted in Palmer, *The Combatant*, 31.

26 Quoted in ibid., 39.

27 Ibid.

28 For a fuller discussion of this phenomenon see D.W. Frank, *Less Than Conquerors: How Evangelicals Entered the Twentieth Century* (Grand Rapids, 1986), 66–75.

29 Quoted in Palmer, *The Combatant*, 40–1.

30 N. Furniss, *The Fundamentalist Controversy, 1918-1931* (New Haven, 1954), 36. This theme is superbly developed in C. Johnston, *McMaster University: The Toronto Years*, 2 vols. (Toronto, 1976), 1:170-203.

31 For information about the Soul Winner's Association, see its Nova Scotia publication, *The Challenge*, found in the Public Archives of Nova Scotia (PANS).

32 PANS, "Daily Programme of the Soul Winner's Festival, 1 July-10 July 1922." Microfilm of some of the printed material used by Gertrude Palmer in her study of Sidey.

33 See *The Challenge* for 1923.

34 Quoted in Palmer, *The Combatant*, 54.

35 Ibid.

36 See Victor Turner, *The Ritual Process: Structure and Anti-Structure* (Ithaca, 1979), 139–40.

37 Quoted in Palmer, *The Combatant*, 56.

38 Quoted in ibid., 58.

39 J. Carpenter, "The Revival of American Fundamentalism," (PHD diss., John Hopkins University, 1984), 5.

40 E.R. Sandeen, *The Roots of Fundamentalism: British and American Millennarianism, 1800-1930* (Chicago, 1970).

41 G.M. Marsden, *Fundamentalism and American Culture: The Shaping of Twentieth-Century Evangelicalism 1870-1925* (New York, 1980).

42 A.T. Doyle, *Front Benches and Back Rooms* (Toronto, 1976), 85–97.

43 See Palmer, *The Combatant*, 78–88.

44 Ibid., 74.

45 Quoted in ibid., 74.

46 Some of the manuscript papers of the Reverend Morris are in the possession of Professor Barry Moody, Acadia University. Professor Moody purchased these and other Morris materials at auction. Other Morris material has recently surfaced in the Hamilton, Ontario, region. Interview with a group of Fellowship Baptist Ministers in Stanley Avenue Baptist Church, Hamilton, 9 April 1987.

47 *United Baptist Year Book 1927* (Truro, 1927), 14.

48 Ibid.

49 Materials found in the Sidey Papers in the AUA.

50 Sidey Papers, AUA.

51 Ibid.

52 It is noteworthy that Mason was to play a key role in orchestrating the anti-Sidey movement at the convention in the 1930s.

53 *Gospel Light*, Kingston, October, 1934.

54 Information about these conferences is to be found in the Sidey Papers, AUA.

55 None of these men is mentioned in *The Acadia Record 1838-1953* (Wolfville, 1953). I have discovered some relevant material in *The United Baptist Year Book 1929* and *The United Baptist Year Book 1930*.

56 See the program for the 1931 conference to be found in the Sidey Papers in the AUA.

57 Court Records, AUA.

58 This is a very important theme in Joel Carpenter, "The Renewal of American Fundamentalism," (PHD diss., John Hopkins University, 1984). See V.L. Brereton, "Protestant Fundamentalist Bible Schools, 1882-1946," (PHD diss., Columbia University, 1981).

59 See the Court Records, AUA.

60 *Gospel Light*, October 1934. See also the *Maritime Baptist*, 13 June 1934.

61 *Gospel Light*, October 1934.

62 Ibid.

63 Ibid.

64 Ibid.

65 Ibid.

66 Court Records, AUA.

67 *Maritime Baptist*, 12 September 1934.

68 Ibid.

69 Ibid.

70 See C.H. Pinnock, "The Modernist Impulse at McMaster University, 1887-1927," in J. Zeman, ed., *Baptists in Canada* (Burlington, 1980), 195.

71 Ibid., 204–5.

72 This conclusion is based on a careful reading of the *Maritime Baptist* during the 1918 to 1939 period. See also *The United Baptist Year Book* for the same period.

73 *Halifax Herald*, 27 May 1935.

74 Ibid., 22 May 1935.

75 *Halifax Chronicle*, 18 September 1935.

76 *The Question*, June 1935. (A microfilm of this Sidey publication is to be found in the PANS.)

77 Ibid., October 1935.

78 Ibid., June 1936.

79 *Halifax Chronicle*, 18 September 1935.

80 *The Question*, July 1935.

81 Ibid., August 1935.

82 Unless otherwise noted, all of the quotations about the Kentville trial used in this section are from the Court Records, AUA.

83 See, for example, *Halifax Herald*, 24 May 1935.

84 Ibid., 27 May 1935.

85 *Acadia Bulletin*, January 1957.

86 These three men, all of whom had connections with Canada, were widely regarded as leading liberal theologians.

87 *Acadia Bulletin*, November 1954. See also S. Spidle, *An Outline of Theology* 2 vols. (1953). These two volumes of lectures were privately printed by Spidle; found in the AUA.

88 *Maritime Baptist*, 25 September 1935.

89 See *The Question*, December 1935.

90 AUA, Minute Book of the Eastern Baptist Association of Nova Scotia, Sydney, 4 July 1935.

91 Ibid.

92 *United Baptist Year Book 1935*, 145.

93 *The Acadia Record 1838-1952*, 54.

94 See the *United Baptist Year Book, 1931-38, 1939-41*.

95 See W. Ellis, "Social and Religious Factors."

96 See the "Records of the Church of Jebogue in Yarmouth," in the PANS.

97 See Marlene Shore, "Carl Dawson and the Research Ideal: The Evolution of a Canadian Sociologist," *Canadian Historical Association Historical Papers* (1985): 73.

98 Quoted in *The Maritime Baptist*, 12 September 1934.

99 *The Question*, December 1935.

100 *Gospel Light*, October 1934.

101 *The Maritime Baptist*, 22 June 1938.

102 See some of the criticism of Sidey in the Sidey Papers, AUA.

103 Quoted in Palmer, *The Combatant*, 160. I have learned a great deal about Sidey's latter years from Mrs George Moody of Wolfville and from Professor Barry Moody of Acadia University.

104 Quoted in Palmer, *The Combatant*, 195.

105 Ibid., 196. I am indebted to Professor Phil Buckner, editor of *Acadiensis*, for permission to use here much of my article originally published in *Acadiensis*.

THREE

1 Quoted in J.D.E. Dozois, "Dr. Thomas Todhunter Shields (1873-1955): In the Stream of Fundamentalism," (BD thesis, McMaster Divinity College, 1963), 57.

2 *Saturday Night*, 11 July 1931.

3 *Maclean's*, 15 June 1949.

4 See Dozois, "Dr. T.T. Shields," p. 130.

5 R.G. Turnbull, *A History of Preaching*, 3 vols. (Grand Rapids, 1974), 3:329–30.

6 See I.H. Murray, *D. Martyn Lloyd-Jones, The First Forty Years: 1899-1939* (Edinburgh, 1984), 272.

7 For a very sympathetic and uncritical view of Shields see L.K. Tarr, *Shields of Canada* (Grand Rapids, 1967).

8 C.A. Russell, "Thomas Todhunter Shields, Canadian Fundamentalist," *Ontario History* 70 (1978): 264. This is, by far, the best short study of T.T. Shields.

9 Ibid., 263.

10 See G.A. Rawlyk, "A.L. McCrimmon, H.P. Whidden, T.T. Shields, Christian Education, and McMaster University," in G.A. Rawlyk, ed., *Canadian Baptists and Christian Higher Education* (Kingston and Montreal, 1988), 31–62; see also W.E. Ellis, "What the Times Demand: Brandon College and Baptist Higher Education in Canada," in ibid., 63–87.

11 Quoted in G.W. Carder, "Controversy in the Baptist Convention, 1908-1929" (BD thesis, McMaster University, 1950), 66.

12 Quoted in L.K. Tarr, "Another Perspective on T.T. Shields," in J.K. Zeman, ed., *Baptists in Canada* (Burlington 1980), 219.

13 Lee Ann Purchase, "T.T. Shields: Devil or Saint?" (Paper, autumn 1986, to be found in the Baptist Archives, McMaster Divinity College), 26.

14 Ibid.

15 Ibid., 26–7.

16 See W.E. Ellis, "Gilboa to Ichabod: Social and Religious Factors in the Fundamentalist-Modernist Schisms Among Canadian Baptists, 1895-1934" *Foundations* 20 (1977): 113.

17 See *Acadiensis* 12, no. 1 (Autumn, 1987): 3–33.

18 Ibid., 32.

19 Palmer, *The Combatant*, 57.

20 J.N. Barnes, *Light and Shadows of Eighty Years* (Saint John, 1911).

21 See the excellent article by G.S. May, "Des Moines University and Dr. T.T. Shields," *Iowa Journal of History* (July 1956): 193–232.

22 C.M. Johnston, *McMaster University: The Toronto Years*, 2 vols. (Toronto, 1976), 1:199.

23 See J. Stackhouse, "Proclaiming the Word: Canadian Evangelicalism Since World War I," (PHD diss., University of Chicago, 1987), 30–2.

24 Interviews with Gertrude Palmer and Hollis Hudson, 5 August 1987.

25 See the Delnay articles in *Central C.B. Quarterly*, Fall 1964; Spring 1965; Summer 1965.

26 Daggett to Shields, 12 February 1924. This letter and the following ones to and from Shields are to be found in the Shields Papers, Jarvis Street Baptist Church, Toronto, Ontario

27 Emphasis added.

28 See Bennett to Shields, 2 January 1926.

29 See J.J. Sidey's autobiography, "The Widow's Mite," in the possession of G.A. Rawlyk.

30 Sidey to Shields, 19 November 1926.

31 T.T. Shields to William Aberhart, 4 August 1926.

32 Russell, "Thomas Todhunter Shields," 272.

33 See also the Daggett letter to Shields, 11 August 1931.

34 Daggett to Shields, 22 November 1934.

35 Shields to Daggett, 5 January 1935.

36 Daggett to Shields, 8 May 1935.

37 Daggett to Shields, 23 August 1935.

38 Shields to Daggett, 15 December 1935.

39 Shields to Sidey, 15 July 1939.

40 Sidey to Shields, 1 October 1936.

41 Shields to Aberhart, 4 August 1926.

42 See Murray, *D. Martyn Lloyd-Jones*, 272.

43 See Mark Parent, "T.T. Shields and the First World War," a paper delivered at the First Baptist Church, Cornwall, 31 April 1988. Paper in possession of G.A. Rawlyk.

Index

THE WINTHROP PICKARD BELL
LECTURES IN MARITIME STUDIES

Hugh MacLennan *On being a Maritime Writer* (1982–83)
William B. Hamilton *Regional Identity: A Maritime Quest* (1983–84)
M. Ross, F. Cogswell and M. Maillet *The Bicentennial Lectures on New Brunswick Literature* (1984)
E.A. Forsey, J.A. Richardson, and G.S. Kealey *Perspective on the Atlantic Canadian Labour Movement and the Working Class Experience* (1985)
J.M. Bumsted *Understanding the Loyalists* (1985–86)
B. Fleming, ed., *Beyond Anger and Longing* (1986–87)
G.W. Rawlyk *Champions of the Truth: Fundamentalism, Modernism, and the Maritime Baptists* (1987–88)